JUDD PUB

Denis Allen J[illegible] born in 1911 in a picturesque village in northern Northamptonshire on the same day that George V was crowned King-Emperor. The only child of a village policeman and his wife – herself the daughter of a police superintendant – his boyhood was marked by many moves to different Northamptonshire villages. Finally settled in Byfield, in the south of the county, he married a girl from the neighbouring village of Woodford Halse, Joan Shrimpton, in 1937. The couple have lived in Byfield ever since, bringing up their two children, and welcoming visits from their seven grandchildren, relations and friends. Denis started his working life as a country postman, cycling many miles each day to the lone farms, and getting to know a variety of local characters. He then began to repair bicycles for a living, soon graduating to car hire and repair. Eventually he built up a business repairing cars, selling petrol and coal, and running a fleet of buses. Now retired, he is a skilful and indefatigable gardener and handiman, and a shrewd observer of the country scene he loves so much.

D.A. Judd

Living In The Country

Life in Rural Northamptonshire from Before the First World War

JUDD PUBLISHING

Published by Judd Publishing
20 Mount Pleasant Road, London NW10 3EL, England

First Published 1991
Second Edition published 1992
Third Edition published 1993

Text design by Kate Judd

Typeset in 12/15 Monotype Bembo
Printed and bound in Great Britain by
The Ipswich Book Company Ltd.

Contents

Chapter 1

The Coronation of a King and the Birth of One of his Subjects: 1911

I was born in a very picturesque and completely unspoilt village in Northamptonshire where the houses were built of soft, golden-brown stone, a colour that always made you think of sun-baked days – even in winter they seemed to glow with hidden warmth. They were topped with generous, golden straw thatch, done as only thatchers who have had their skills and know-how handed down by their forefathers could, in the traditional Northamptonshire style. Thatching always seemed to run in families and all trade secrets were closely guarded and handed down from father to son. They felt a pride in their work (no hurrying by with eyes down and fearing winter storms for them) – indeed, on a Sunday morning they would stand and admire their handiwork. 'We did that,' they would say with pride. They would know each other's work as they travelled through the county and villages around – 'Jim Hartwell did that,' 'Percy Brookes did that,' as sure as if they had signed their names on a board and pinned it to the ridge.

This combination of stone and thatch put together to build sturdy cottages arranged in a most unconventional manner, would appear to follow no pattern or design, but always looked right and in the best positions for the sun and to keep out the cold winds. There were no problems with flooding and the like, and there was always a good vegetable garden with room for a pig-sty and somewhere for a few hens to scratch about. These were the essentials for the generations of families that lived in them over the years; an ideal setting, completely unspoilt by the Northampton–Bedford turnpike that wandered past the church, the village green, over the crossroads and past the village stocks and out through the parish, quite unhurried. Plenty of time for hens to bather in the dusty surface and dogs to dream their dreams on the grass bordering the rutted, untarred road – none of your feet-aching tarmac strips in those days.

The old men of the village had favourite places to meet (under the Cross Tree or outside the blacksmith's shop), but on this June day, where better than the seats and tables outside the inn, drinking the new King's health in suitable local brewed ale (no chemical muck in those days). I have so many times been told by my old friends in later years, as we watched our local team at cricket – 'Why, boy, if a fly settled on the rings on the table left by your pot in those days, it couldn't fly off – pulled its feet off – so strong, like treacle.' Is it any wonder England was great? What beer, what men!

We had more than the usual number of large houses and halls in the beautiful, unspoilt surrounding countryside that made up our parish. The village consisted of a church, complete with rectory, and a church school for the village children, a large working flour mill, the water driven by the river Nene, a blacksmith's forge, carpenter's and undertaker's premises, a shoemaker, a butcher and a sweet shop which stocked everything under the sun. There were several large farms and a thriving market garden. These were all beneficial for the working population. I think the doctor came from another village, making his calls by pony and trap.

My father came to live here as the new, young village bobby, fresh out of training, his first posting in fact. Whilst he did his training he married his superintendent's daughter, my mother-to-be. This was just as well, as it is not always easy to be the wife of a policeman and she had been brought up as a policeman's daughter. In those days a policeman had to find his own house, and my father said to his special constable and helpmate, who had lived in the village all his life, 'Walt, get that little cottage next door to yours and a piece of allotment, and I'll be happy.' Walt somehow worked the oracle and this is how I came to be born just across the road from the church to the sound of the church bells ringing for the Coronation service for the new King.

Our cottage was only a few yards from the belfry tower, so on a June day during the hottest and driest summer on record (1911), and on one of the hottest days of that year, there was a young mother-to-be found struggling in the confines of her small, cramped, furnace-hot bedroom, to the din of bells ringing non-stop, rung by keen and enthusiastic men who had been waiting for this joyous, flag-strewn and beribboned day.

Is it any wonder that the village midwife was at a loss? Should she shut the bedroom window to try and keep out the joyous sound of bells, or let in much-needed fresh air for the young mother in her first confinement? My mother said to me in later years, 'How I wished you would hurry up or they would shut up.' However, it seems that I compromised by waiting till the church service started and the ringing abated before putting in an appearance, much to the relief of the two hardworking women in the bedroom, one skilled by years of practice in bringing hundreds of babies into the world, and for the other a new experience and one never to be forgotten – 'You did make my eyes run – over 9lbs, fat and lazy, you rascal.'

It would appear from the midwife's remarks a little later that I did not remain lazy for many minutes after being bathed and put in my long gown, trussed up as was the fashion in those days. Just time now for the old midwife to get out the best and very precious tea service, not so long ago a prized wedding present, to make herself and my mother a well-deserved cup of tea – 'None of your everyday china for a Coronation and birthday, we will do the job properly.' A few minutes later, the nurse rushed upstairs to mother, 'Oh, that baby is so strong and active, he kicked one of your best cups out of my hand and has broken it!' Not a bad start in life to overpower a village midwife who was as strong as an ox, with muscles developed by tending sick people, endless washing by hand, and miles of walking every day. How my father laughed!

My father, I understand, kept out of the way by going out to show the uniform and to keep an eye on things in the village, dashing back to old Walt Rose's cottage next door and waiting for little Mrs Rose to keep popping back with progress reports.

'If it's a boy we'll wet his head when we drink the Royal toast tonight,' my father said, and according to Mrs Rose, who was a dear, meek and mild lady, 'I was quite shocked, it was no way for a policeman and his special constable to behave.' Long live the King! Good luck to the baby!

It has never ceased to amaze me in after years, when I heard about that terrible year of drought. There was no feed for the cattle and sheep, the trees were lopped for miles around for fodder, the earth all cracked up and water being carted from drying-up rivers. Brooks were all finished, and even if you dug a hole in the bed no water filtered in. There were dust clouds being blown about and everywhere had a tatty look. Our kind and so needy neighbours brought drops of precious water, saved I don't know how, in their milk cans for the new baby, and kept the water that filtered into the village pump overnight for the young and frail. Surely a lesson to us all in these supposedly enlightened and advanced days.

Walter Rose, who was the head miller at the huge and fearsome water-mill in the village, was a tower of strength to the young policeman. Mrs Rose was a little grey wren of a lady – petite and round, with her hair scraped back, a happy shining face, and a very gentle nature. Just the opposite to her husband Walt, who was at least six foot tall with large hands and feet, and not an ounce of surplus flesh on his strong frame. Mrs Rose helped my mother to cope with an antiquated, stubborn fire-grate used for cooking, and helped to coax an old wood-burning wash-boiler, that had to be filled by hand with buckets of water from a pump yards away, to do the weekly wash.

The Roses had a daughter, Eve, who was a few years older than me, and I was just what she wanted, a real, live doll. My mother told me that as soon as I began to crawl about and was past the fragile stage, Eve set about me in her quaint, old-fashioned way. She dressed and undressed me, washed, bathed, powdered and polished me for hours on end, saying 'This is a little boy – I'm a little girl.' My mother, who had nine brothers and sisters, knew that babies were pretty tough creatures, and would come to very little harm if kept at ground level and out of the fire; she got on with her housework and sewing, and let the little mother beaver away. Was there ever such a spoilt baby? I can remember being put in the pram, taken out of the pram, going shopping and down to the meadows for picnics with other little mothers – food wiped off my face with spit on a dock leaf – daisy-chained and milkmaid-garlanded, both me and my pram.

Eve took me to her school and Sunday school, and sometimes, if I was good, to church, but the trip that frightened me most was when we made the long trek to her father's place of work, the mill. I can see it now with its roaring mill-race, spray and foam everywhere and such a noise that you could not hear yourself cry. If we had brought her father's dinner basket, we went inside. What a place of torture! Whirling, whining wheels grinding away, flails flapping, steel chains rattling and clanking, trapdoors opening and shutting, sacks being whirled about by white monsters in the shape of men. We ducked under shafts rotating with flapping belts on pullies and, still keeping our heads down, we would creep along dimly lit corridors festooned with miles and miles of cobwebs covered in flour, to a huge room where every kind of activity was going on. A large white ghost would come walking towards us and Eve would say, 'Dad, we've brought your snap.' Then we would go with this white man, who I now recognised by his hearty laugh, and make our way to the quiet part of the mill grounds where there was a lovely calm mill-pond, and we would be taken in a flat-bottomed boat for a row. This was heaven, and made all my shivers worth while.

When I came back to the village as a big boy to see Walter and Mrs Rose and Eve, and went fishing with Walter and one or two village boys, I was always glad to hurry past the mill, always remembering the times when my father and Walter, together with other men, had pulled out of the mill-race poor, unfortunate people who had either fallen in by accident, or more often, by design, such was the attraction of the fast-moving water.

Our frequent visits to the Squire's house were a revelation. My father, in the course of his duties, had to make and keep various appointments (known in the Force as a point). After seeing the Squire and his good lady, and making sure all was well, he went with their blessing to see the head gardener. My mother and I went to the back of the house to the kitchen to see the cook and housekeeper who were good friends of mother's. What a colossal room – big, black, shining ranges along one side, dressers covered with copper pots and pans, and rows and rows of colourful dishes and plates. The shelves were laden with all kinds of jars, and there were lots of young girls to-ing and fro-ing in their various uniforms. In the centre of the room was an enormous, scrubbed, whiter than white table and chairs. The flour bins, were all scrubbed white too. The cook had an easy chair on one side of the monster of a fireplace, and the chair on the other side was for visitors – my mother in this case. But of all the things that took my eye was a square tin on the mantleshelf covered with pictures of Lord Kitchener, which cook would get down at last and from it take out a chocolate finger biscuit. 'For the boy, I hope he doesn't get himself plastered,' she would say. I couldn't care less – I couldn't keep my eyes off that tin. I've never tasted such chocolate biscuits since.

These regular visits to large houses and mansions were not only in the line of duty for a village constable. He was also instructed in no uncertain manner by his senior officers – 'You work hand in hand with the gamekeepers and your job will be made easier.' A good keeper and under-keeper knew all the shady characters, like poachers, and more or less when to expect them. Also, keepers were out most of the night, sometimes all night, tending their pheasants and partridges, protecting them from predators, both animal and human. This was all done with stealth and patience – what better allies could you have than these two custodians of other people's property and safety, in the lonely wooded areas found in our lovely countryside.

The owners of these large houses and estates were invariably justices of the peace, magistrates, maybe the Lord Lieutenant of the County, and quite often a Member of Parliament. If you wanted to get on in your job and not be moved to a less idyllic area, these country gentlemen could not be ignored and the best attention your job called for should be given unreservedly to one and all. County squires were also understanding when it came to distributing largesse; 'Go and see the cook, she's got something for your wife,' as indeed she had – basins of dripping, a slice of game pie, freshly baked bread, and so on. What a godsend for a young couple who, after the rent was paid, had twenty-four shillings a week left to live on. 'Go and see the head gardener,' who found us grapes, peaches, or apricots, both in season and sometimes out of season. Strawberries, too, were plentiful. Often the butler or footman would offer a glass of beer or, in bad weather, a nip of whisky, to keep out the chill night air.

It went without saying that a young, country-born, intelligent and very smart young man like my father (three years in a crack artillery regiment before undertaking his police training), would try and please and give no cause for complaint. Life would not have been so easy in one of the small boot and shoe towns, where the cobblers were a law unto themselves, most independent and aggressive, and who worked when they felt like it. No easy task for the police at weekends and on a Cobbler's Monday. They invariably started work on a Tuesday, after a hectic weekend.

There was always the odd rabbit hanging up outside the keeper's cottage for anyone who wanted it. When the big shoots took place, and all the local gentry and farmers met for an organised slaughter, the village men who were not in regular employment volunteered like a shot to be taken on by the keepers. Apart from the excitement of the day's sport, a day's wages was to be earned, backed up with liberal helpings of bread and cheese and a harvest bottle (made of wood), full of home-brewed beer which was filled up again at the end of the day and taken home to be shared with the family.

Both keepers and policeman knew very well that a few birds, that had supposedly got away, were hidden in the bracken to be picked up later that night. They knew how hard times were for the village folk who were not sheltered by the big houses; very little regular work, just seasonable jobs such as harvesting, threshing, haymaking and beating for the shoots – not enough to keep large families on (no dole in those days). After the day's massive slaughter of game, what did a few birds matter? Stern looks were directed towards the beaters and words like, 'By God, don't you let me catch you doing it again, you know the master is no fool and he is a magistrate, he's got you lot weighed up.' There might also be added, 'We are all going up to the servants' hall tonight for the shoot supper which will last until about 10 o'clock. We don't want to see you lot when we are on our way home.' The advice was also given, in a roundabout sort of way: 'If you get really down on your luck ask to see the master or mistress, not the agent – he will have no time for you, he must make the estate pay or he will be for the high jump himself.' By obeying these age-old rules, life was made easier for all, not least the village policeman, who did not want to summons these men who, as he knew, were the salt of the earth.

My mother told me that she was talking to one such dear old man who was sitting on the doorstep of his cottage, warming his bones in the sun, when she heard a strange and unrecognisable sound in the sky and, much to her amazement, saw what could only be an aeroplane.

'Look,' she said to the old man, 'an aeroplane.'

'An aeroplane,' he said, 'I've been looking at that, my gal, for some time. I thought it were an old 'arran,' (heron); and, indeed, so sedately did those first planes fly that the old fellow was quite entitled to think it was a heron when seen through those age-dimmed eyes (very few people could afford spectacles in those days).

It would seem that this lone plane was a scout prospecting for a safe and manageable air route for the air race that was to take place shortly. The first we knew of this race was when Father came home very excited – 'We are going to have dozens of aeroplanes land in Farmer Luck's big field just outside the village next week.' (The King's Cup Air Race, I think he said.) 'They are drafting in more of our men to help me, you see precautions must be taken, the public must be kept back out of harm's way – children could get their heads cut off with those spinning propellers.' He told us that his superior officers and many local bigwigs would be there, there would be tents, vans and the occasional motor car would be seen; it would be a day to remember for the rest of our lives. How right he was: here I am over seventy-five years later still remembering as clearly as if it were yesterday – those weird, noisy, floppy things coming out of the sky before our very eyes. I can remember the fear, coupled with excitement, I felt as I was lifted up to touch the flimsy, smelly canvas and wire and, dare I say it, string contraption. Imagine my horror when my father, who carried me around on his shoulders, handed me up to a strangely dressed man with huge glass eyes on his cap, who sat me in this big round hole with levers inside, so unlike anything I had seen before. What a fuss I kicked up until I was handed back to the safe and strong arms of the law I knew so well. You could get some idea of how flimsy those flying machines were, and how unreliable their engines could be, by the course being plotted in only twenty-one mile hops, I am told. When the time came for take-off – I think it was the next day because I remember going up to the field twice – what a performance! Noise, smoke, planes moving around the field, some unable to move at all, others wobbling off into the sky in the direction of Northampton. The crowds cheered and waved goodbye and a good day was had by one and all. My trip across the Atlantic in later years in a jumbo jet with more people inside than were on that field all those years ago, was so calm and tame in comparison.

All this aerial activity by those fearless men in their flying machines was, without a doubt, in readiness in case the rumours and counter-rumours of trouble in Europe became reality. These war clouds were so unreal and must surely blow away. That new King of mine, so friendly with his cousin, the Kaiser, who was so often in England visiting his relations, our Royal family, attending the races, both horse and yacht, and spending several weeks here on army manoeuvres. He spent a lot of time in and out of our beautiful Northamptonshire villages, staying and dining with our county squires. It just could not happen – a lot of warmongers writing in the papers – let's just get on with our lives and not worry.

My father, who was on the army reserve force (three years in the army, seven years on the reserve), was not so sure that war was all that far away. 'They are moving me to another village in the county; we will not be there many months before I am called up,' he would say to old Walt Rose. 'I'm so happy here with you lot, I don't want to move and maybe join my regiment – I like it here with my friends. What about my garden and allotment?'

'Allotment,' said Walter. 'Allotment – your back's too straight for allotments; the times I have found your spade stuck in the ground on your plot and you nowhere in sight. If I hadn't dug a few rows across and back it would not have been done in time for planting.'

I must say that Walt was right, because my father made a wonderful soldier. He fought right through the war, from 1914 to the army occupation of part of Germany in 1919. After this he returned, and became once more a village bobby.

Chapter 2

Moving to Another Village,
and Gathering War Clouds

I well remember the hustle and bustle of moving house, my mother packing her precious things in boxes and small tin baths, remarking how many more things she had now than when she came as a bride those few years ago. 'Your high chair,' she would tell me, 'cost us twenty-four shillings and sixpence from Northampton, a complete week's wages. Mr Luck, the carrier, brought it home.' And, indeed, it may have cost all of one week's wages, but my word, what good value. I used it until I could no longer get into it and it then went to my younger cousin and was returned to me for our son and daughter. It spent a good number of years with my wife's sister's three children, coming back home to do service for our seven grandchildren. The youngest one of the seven, even when too grown up to sit in a high chair with a potty in the seat, was quite happy to pull a lever and make it into a rocking chair on which to have fun and games. What a tribute to Victorian craftsmanship. There are years of service left in it, and it should go the rounds once more if today's mothers can put up with it in their up-to-date houses.

To get back to the excitement of moving house. On the appointed morning a huge miller's-type covered wagon drew up outside our cottage, pulled by two draught-horses, and our furniture and bits and pieces were loaded up for the journey to our new home. After the wagon had left, my mother, knowing that it would not reach its destination before late afternoon, said, 'I am going to scrub this old cottage out from top to bottom – I'll see that the new people will have no cause for complaint and will be unable to say I was dirty.' The motto of the women of this generation was 'Cleanliness is next to Godliness', and so it remained throughout my mother's life. Heaven help a spider that dared to weave a web in our house.

When our old cottage was spick and span, my father went and fetched the pony and trap we had hired to take us on. We knew we should overtake our furniture wagon before it completed its journey to our new home, and so we did, and we were there waiting to help unload. So seldom did village people move in those days that crowds of children stood in a circle around the wagon and there were many Oohs! and Ahs! as different items were lifted down and carried in. I remember some almighty Ahs! when my father's Windsor armchair and the six kitchen chairs that went with it were unloaded. I felt they were a trifle light in colour, but not so the onlookers – they caused quite a stir. My mother told me, years after this move, that she gave 10½ d each for the kitchen chairs and 5/– for the Windsor chair, which our daughter has to this day.

It did not take us long to settle in. My father soon made himself known to one and all and the cosy pattern of quiet village life began all over again. Not so for me. Not just afternoon school as in the village I had left, but full-time schooling from now on. My father, wearing his uniform, took me to school and registered me, produced my birth certificate, and off I went to join my new class. As I looked around the room, boys were putting up their fists at me and my tummy turned over – what was I in for? When the bell rang for playtime, I soon found out! I was grabbed, thrust against the wall and all kinds of dire threats were made about what would happen to a policeman's kid if he told tales to his dad.

When they were sure that I had got the message, I was measured back to back with other boys until they found one the same height as me. We were taken out into the centre of the playground and made to face one another. A line was drawn between us and I was told to toe it, then spit over it, and when my opponent had done the same, let battle commence! This is where I came into my own. I was a sturdy, strong boy for my age, and I more than held my own. When I went home for my dinner, all cuts and bruises, my mother was shocked.

'Look at him,' she said to my father, when he came in, 'look at him – clothes dirty, knees bleeding, face scratched.'

'Don't worry,' said my father, 'the headmaster saw me and told me what had happened.'

Apparently, he had watched out of the school window to make sure that I came to no harm. It was the custom of the school, and indeed the whole village, to draw a line, toe it and spit over it and then start fighting. A bit off-putting for a new boy – I was to witness it many times with youths and, indeed, grown men when they became bored, standing in groups on street corners. This custom was probably handed down from feudal times.

There was a marked change in the life of the village a few months after we had settled in. People were standing in groups, whispering and shaking their heads and looking worried. For we children, life was much the same, fishing, bird-nesting, playing on the farms and getting into mischief. It was not until I went home one day and found my father sitting in his armchair, and my mother in tears, that I realised how serious things were. I ran to my father and sat on his knee and my mother put her arms round us, crying bitterly. 'Don't worry,' said my father, 'it will all be over in six months.' (How wrong can you be?) The dreaded reservist call-up papers had arrived and war was about to be declared.

A change was soon to be noticed in the peaceful, unhurried life of the village. The gentry donned their uniforms and joined their old regiments, often taking with them their butlers and valets who, nine times out of ten, had been with them in the services before, when it was the done thing to do. Young and enthusiastic men walked the ten miles to Northampton to enlist – 'We must hurry up or it will all be over,' – six months at the outside was the general opinion. 'I should just like to get a crack at Jerry!' Poor lads, little did they know. Month by month more and more men from the village disappeared and the women took on men's jobs, leaving us children to such untold freedom, it was too good to be true! The policeman was in the army, most of the school governors were also missing, our young and strict junior teacher had disappeared, and a shy girl called Kate had been sent to replace him. The kindly and aged headmaster was deeply involved in the sport of kings, and I can see the blackboard now, covered with the names of horses and racing formulas, whilst he held earnest discussions with the older lads, many of whom had grooms and ex-jockeys for fathers. What a paradise for unruly kids! One of the methods of getting us warm in winter, as heating was very limited, was to take us out to the playground, make us link arms four or five abreast, form a large circle and go round the playground chanting:

> There was a jolly miller who lived by himself,
> As the wheel went round he made his wealth,
> One hand in his pocket, the other in his bag,
> As the wheel went round he made his grab.

As we sang, we went faster and faster, stamping our feet on the last word of each line with an almighty crash. In no time our toes were warm and our cheeks glowing. On one occasion we were sent out to do this on our own, unsupervised. As we went round, some wag among us changed the 'miller' for 'Kate' – 'Kate, Kate, shit on a plate. Kate, Kate, shit on a plate', and in no time at all the whole school took it up. Out rushed the old headmaster, cane in hand. I'd never seen him so upset before, and he slashed and lashed us, helped by other grown-ups, I know not who, until we were a disorganised rabble. The next day someone came out from the county town, the school attendance officer, I think, and one by one we had to go into the cloakroom for our punishment. Poor Kate! Poor Backside! After a short time our Kate disappeared, to be replaced by a more matronly lady who would stand no nonsense, and at the least spot of trouble would send us to the head for the cane.

After we had been punished, we were not allowed to go back into class but had to stand in the corridor until it was time to go home – 'I will not have you back in class, you wicked boy!' she would say. What a golden opportunity to go straight out of school and hide until it was time to go home – no wonder I had the best collection of birds' eggs for a boy of my age in the school.

Thinking of birds' eggs reminds me of how we used to earn money and at the same time have some fun with the clap nets. The thatch on our cottages was so low and sloping and riddled with holes that sparrows nested in it. With the consent of the owners (they were only too glad to be rid of the mischievous birds because of the damage they did), two of the bigger boys would climb on to the roof and spread the nets over the holes and we younger boys would beat the thatch with long, thin canes, shining our bull's-eye lantern. Out would come the sparrows' to be caught in the net and sold for a halfpenny each at the cobbler's shop. This buying of sparrows may seem rather odd nowadays, and also very cruel, but there was a Government scheme to rid the countryside of vermin. The going rate, as far as I can remember, was one halfpenny for rats, mice and sparrows, and one penny for twelve sparrows' eggs. Needless to say, we did not deliver the complete rat or mouse, only their tails. You will often find in old parish church records more or less the same arrangements for freeing the church of livestock. This may seem very harsh to us in these days, but you know, times were hard and people had to be hard to survive – look at your pig, which you treated like a brother, at times even better, and then you ate him!

The old cobbler, who collected the gruesome bits and pieces, would sit working away in his shop, grumbling about having to leave off to see us, and grudgingly paying out the coppers to our leader. Sometimes, one of the bigger boys, whilst we held the cobbler's attention, would creep into the shed at the back of the shop and grab a handful of tails to sell them again to the unsuspecting man. The silent laughter, and cunning looks, over this prank, would go the rounds wherever youths congregated. I have often wondered how the old cobbler balanced his till. I know he was very fond of his pint – he may have thought he had miscounted somehow.

There was also another Government scheme to help with the war effort, and this one we really enjoyed. The whole school and, more or less, the whole village, would go blackberrying and also collect rose-hips and conkers by the bushel – that beat school any day of the week. The blackberries were mixed with apples for jam for the troops, the rose-hips were used for medicine, and the conkers, we were told, went to make gunpowder. Whether this was true or not, I don't know, but it was fun. We must have worked hard one year collecting our jam-making material, because the whole village was invited to the Hall by the squire's wife, who's husband and son were at the front. Her son won one of the first VC's for bravery in the air, if not the first. (More about him later.)

This day out at the Hall was like a shot in the arm to weary and worried folk. The Women's Voluntary Service helped to organise the stalls and tea tent, and the men from the village helped with the sports and sideshows – it was almost like a village fête, without having to dig into your pockets. I am sure we all benefited by this get-together. When it came to tea-time, we children sat at long trestle tables, whereupon huge, inch-thick slices from new cottage loaves, cut straight across, with *no* butter (butter was very scarce and very strictly rationed), but plastered with about a quarter of an inch thickness of the most delicious home-made strawberry jam, were put before us. Even to this day, when I have strawberry jam which my wife makes so well, I think of those hunks of new bread, no butter, but lashings of jam. Delicious!

The railway station was about two miles out of the village, and we used to walk down to see the trains which ran very infrequently. We knew the times of the trains by heart, and it was a pleasure to see other people and, who knows? we might see one of our local soldier boys coming home on leave, and if so, we would carry his kitbag and run alongside of him, trying to keep in step, and asking him all kinds of questions about the war; poor boy, I don't think he wanted to talk; he had a few days leave in which to rest and forget. I am sure that at the back of his mind was the thought, 'Will I ever see this again?' Life was not long on an average, in the County infantry regiments.

What necessities were not brought in to us by the carrier's cart, had to come by rail to our station, and there was a constant to-ing and fro-ing with carts, traps and bone-shaker bicycles.

I was friendly with a farmer's son, who lived outside the village. One day we were asked by his mother to get the old donkey and go and meet his sister Mary, who would be arriving by train from boarding school. 'You can take the donkey for her luggage,' she said. It took us some time to catch the donkey which had been in the field with the horses ever since Mary had gone away to school. It valued its freedom, but it could not outwit we two boys, and we soon had a halter on him and took him out past the farmhouse and into the lane leading to the village and so on to the station. As we passed the farmhouse, my friend's mother shouted, 'Lead him, now. No getting up.' But have you ever known two boys to walk when they could ride? As soon as we were out of sight of the farm, we both mounted the donkey and away we jogged through the village. All went well until we reached the steep hill which led to the station, when Neddy stopped dead, and, try as we may, he could not be budged and eventually lay down. We could not get him up, and as we could see the train coming, we had to leave him. We met sister Mary and walked back up the hill. Old Ned still lay there, he hadn't moved an inch, and though we tried our hardest, we couldn't get him to budge. Now I've told you how cruel and unfeeling country children could be in those days. We noticed that the old donkey had been kicked by a horse (no doubt he had been tormenting the horses). Aha! this was his Achilles' heel – one smart tap on the bruise and up and away went Neddy, we kids after him, trying to take turns to ride.

On my way to see an old uncle of mine, who lived into his mid-nineties, I go past the site of the old station – no platforms now, no tracks, just a level-crossing gate that is not used, and I think of poor Neddy and those soldier boys we used to meet. This long-lived uncle dwelled there for many years in our village, and he often says to me, 'Boy, do you remember this, do you remember that?' and he tells us of his fights and adventures there many years ago. My son and his three sons listen, spellbound. I'll try and remember to tell you some of his stories later on.

Between the village and the railway station at the bottom of our hill there was a bridge, under which ran a swift-running brook with crystal-clear water. It was the custom to drive the carts and traps through this brook, between the side of the bridge and the hedge, to soak and swell up the sun-dried wooden wheels with their huge iron tyres, and so make them firm and sound for the rough ground. Also, the men on their way back from the fields would let the strong and sturdy cart-horses cool their great hairy legs and feet in this ice-cold stream, and quench their thirst. Years of such practice widened the brook until it was a good-sized pool with a hard, pebbly bottom, with water 12 to 18 inches in depth. What a place, out of their parents' sight, for boys to paddle and, after a while, get more venturesome, take all of their clothes off and lay down in the shallow pool, splash about and pretend to swim. Before long, attracted by our shouts and laughter, would come the girls; they would lean over the bridge, shrieking and making lewd and unflattering remarks about our personal anatomy, much to the annoyance of the bigger boys, who would splash them with water and tell them to go away. 'Leave us alone,' they would shout, all to no avail. Terrific horseplay would develop between the sexes, and in the end, one or two of the older boys would look fierce and threaten the girls. 'We'll have a look at yours, Molly Sykes, and yours Betty Woods,' and out of the water they would dash in their birthday suits, chasing the screaming girls who would run into a nearby field full of rush-grass and almost covered with the pretty little flowers we called milkmaids, with patches of celandines dotted here and there.

Whether the girls, who set off at great speed with their straw hats and long plaits flying in the wind, and their long white pinafores and long skirts pulled up, showing their black stockings and strong boots, were ever caught and inspected, I shall never know. All I do know is, as they trooped back, hot and bothered, over the bridge, they would shout, 'We shall be down again tomorrow.' We would continue with our water-sport (swimming, we thought it was), until the men came home from the fields, sitting side-saddle on their huge mounts, and stopping to let them drink their fill. Some of the old men would advise us to dress and run home, 'You're getting blue in the face and covered with goose pimples.' This good advice we chose to ignore, as is the way of youth. It wasn't until the horses had gone, invariably after they had drunk, either urinated or did far worse in the water, that we got out – all very hygienic!

Talking of water and hygiene reminds me of the drinking-water supply for a row of cottages situated on a slope in our village. Opposite the cottages running water was piped down the ditch in large stone culverts. Every so often a square, shallow well was built, with a hinged wooden cover that was nearly always left open, allowing dust and all kinds of rubbish to blow in. No one seemed to mind and the cottagers would fasten their buckets to a long pole, rather like a shepherd's crook, and draw out the water which they took home to make the tea etc. These wells had a fascination for we boys and on the way home from school we often searched them for frogs and threw stones in the water. But one day we disgraced ourselves and stood weeing into the water, when a cottage door burst open and out rushed an old lady, brandishing a large carving knife, and shouting 'You little devils – I'll cut off your willies!' She looked so cross, I felt sure she meant it. Home I rushed, burst into the house, slammed and bolted the back door, ran crying to my mother and clung to her like grim death.

'Whatever is wrong – do tell me,' said Mother.

'It's old Granny Copson, she's going to cut our willies off for weeing down her well.'

'I'm not a bit surprised,' said my mother, 'don't ever do that again!' and indeed, it was many a week before I dared go past Granny Copson's cottage. I went the long way round to school for a long time.

The field covered in rush-grass and milkmaids close to the brook was a favourite place for nesting plovers and we used to hunt for these dark brown pointed eggs, mottled with black markings, for food. We would roll them up in the bottom of our jerseys to keep them out of sight and meet at a pre-arranged spot. The bigger boys would soon get a fire going, lighting it with their home-made tinder boxes. We cooked the eggs on a spade or a piece of metal held over the fire, and when they were more or less ready, we spread them on a slice of bread and wolfed them down – the things that slip down a healthy, growing lad's throat have to be seen to be believed! There were all kinds of hedgerow fruits, crab apples, swedes and turnips out of the fields, potatoes dug up and cooked, and raids made on the parson's mulberry trees. How we were missing our fathers and the young men of the village to keep us in order – we more or less ran wild.

You may wonder about the tinder-box method of getting a light to start a fire going and ask, why not a match? Matches were very scarce during the First World War, even more so than during the Second World War, when cigarette lighters were made on the side in factories and workshops. Comedians would joke: 'We've had a good week at our factory – we've turned out 5,000 lighters and one aeroplane!' As I have said, matches were very scarce indeed. The most popular were called Wax Vestas and were made of cotton dipped in wax, with a red top. These were very often carried in a flat waterproof box attached to your watch chain (I still have one of my uncle's boxes – he was killed in the Great war). Other matches were sulphurous smelling, spluttering things. One match, I remember, you lit and blew out, and lit again, quite a number of times. All of these were very scarce indeed. Naturally, the old men brought out their tinder boxes, and we copied the design with the aid of a metal cigarette box, a broken file from the blacksmith or farm, some saltpetre from the grocer and we used either unravelled rope to make tow or some old rag. Now we wanted a flint and we knew just the place to find it. This was the driveway on the Squire's estate, where there were hundreds and hundreds of round flint pebbles just for the taking. We would choose a good one, split it, and hey presto, we could now strike the flint with the file, sparks would fly on to the saltpetre soaked tow, then, by gently blowing, we had fire. So much more fun than a match!

My father told me in after years that the Squire's son used to tear up and down this drive with an aeroplane propeller fastened to the front of his car, putting the fear up all and sundry. This was before the war, and my father had to tell him, 'Billy, you must not come out on to the road with that contraption – you will cut someone's head off,' but, I was told, he did make trips to the village frightening everyone he met. What a lad! He joined the flying corps as soon as possible, went to France and either won the first or second Flying Force VC. He was killed in action over enemy lines. How brave and how tragic. Afterwards, we boys often crept up to the house and peered inside the coach-house to look at Billy's mechanical marvels. The boisterous bravado left us and we felt so subdued and so very sad.

The very first German prisoner of war that I saw was when a troop came marching down the village high street, escorted by two or three British soldiers with fixed bayonets. I expect they were going to work on the farms in the area. They looked so unreal to me, with their round pill-box hats, blue-grey uniforms with huge red patches sewn on in different places and tall black jackboots, very heavily soled and heeled with hobnails. What a loud, tramping noise they made as they marched in step, really quite smart, through the village. When they came through the next morning, the women were waiting for them with cat-calls and jeers, throwing whatever they could lay their hands on – one woman even threw a bucket of water. The British guards tried to put a stop to all this, but it was impossible without hurting the women, and so the taunting went on day after day for some time. So many of those women had lost husbands and sons so you can understand how they felt. After this, whenever I saw a German prisoner, if only working on a farm, seemingly quite happy and contented (glad to be alive and out of the war, I don't doubt), my tummy turned over.

This fear of those strangely patch-marked foreign men could have easily caused a serious accident for me and the baker's son. It happened like this: the baker delivered bread to a lot of villages and outlying farms, using two bakers' carts, one pulled by a staid old pony which the son drove, and the other by a young, high-stepping mare driven with pride by his father, who also used her in his trap for fast trips to Northampton and for taking the family out. I often helped the son on his delivery round – I went for the ride mostly.

On this particular day, when we were mucking out and getting the horses ready, harnessing them and putting them in the carts ready for loading up with bread etc., the boy's mother came out and said, 'Reg, you will have to do Dad's round today, he's not well. Young Bert will do yours.' Reg was thrilled to drive this high-stepper and he said to me, 'You come with me to hold her whilst I'm delivering.' We quickly loaded up and off we set at a cracking pace (no doubt showing off a bit). When we were descending a steep hill about two miles out of the village, we saw about a dozen of these strange German prisoners of war working in the fields. Looking up and seeing us, they waved their arms and hoes and started running towards us, shouting and obviously trying to cut us off. Remembering what had happened to them when they came down our high street, we were scared stiff. Reg stood up, grabbed the driving whip and hit the lively mare such a crack. I don't expect she had ever been touched with a whip before and away she went, kicking like mad. As her hooves struck the cart, so she kicked more and finally got her leg over the traces and down we went. I was flung out, the cart tipped over into the ditch, bread flying all over the place, and the mare was down and still kicking. But to make matters worse, as I lay dazed, I could see these fierce Germans rushing towards us, and everyone knew they ate babies! What they would do to a nice juicy boy, I dreaded to think.

Two of the prisoners reached down, picked me up and stood me on my feet and brushed me down, jabbering away all the time. I looked for Reg – he was also being helped up. The other prisoners were attending the mare. One sat on her head to hold her still, others were disentangling the harness and hooking her out and in no time at all the cart was on its wheels, the mare between the shafts and the spilt bread loaded back in the baskets. We tried to thank them but could not make ourselves understood. Then, all of a sudden, the penny dropped – they had waved to stop us in order to buy a loaf, not to eat us! After that episode I was no longer frightened of Germans. As a matter of fact, about two years later, one taught me to ride a bicycle.

At weekends and during the school holidays I enjoyed my trips on the baker's cart. The homely country women made you so welcome. 'Don't bother to knock, just shout "Baker", and come in. We usually have three loaves every time you call, a dough cake and a dozen halfpenny buns for the weekend,' etc., etc. 'If we're not here, just leave them.' It never occurred to them to lock the door until bedtime. How times have changed over the years. Their cottages shone with brass and copper, and there were all kinds of trinkets, handed down, I expect, from one generation to another. There was nearly always a wooden chest, some quite plain and cheaply made, but others obviously of some value.

When we went to the lone farms, we would be questioned about the goings-on in the village, often given letters to post and asked to do all kinds of errands. Reg, who was a lot older than me, would play all kinds of pranks on unsuspecting customers. One of his favourite tricks when we went up the drives of houses and farms, was to get off the seat on top of the box, thread the reins through two ventilating holes in the front, open the doors at the rear of the box and we would then get in with the bread, driving the horse unseen from inside the cart. The good people would see the baker's cart unattended, catch the horse and we would hear them say, 'I don't think he has bolted.' 'No, I reckon he's come on his own whilst Reg has been gossiping. Let's tie him up, they'll soon be along.' All the time this was going on we were nearly bursting. 'Well,' would say the farmer's wife, 'we might as well get our bread out,' opening the doors at the back, and out we would spring, often receiving a good thump for playing such a silly trick.

Another bit of devilment that Reg would get up to, and which involved me, was pinching some of the parson's little red, juicy apples which hung over a very high wall at the side of the road, impossible to reach without a ladder and quite safe from most children, but not Reg, who thought up a scheme. 'I'll drive as close to the wall as I can, without stopping, you reach up, grab as many as you can and we'll be off.' This worked well for some days and was great fun, but it got increasingly more difficult to reach the apples as we had taken all the bottom ones. 'Stand on the seat – that will do the trick,' said Reg. So on the seat I got and around the corner drove Reg at a spanking pace, with me balancing precariously on my perch. I reached up to make my grab, misjudged the height, got tangled in the branches and was swept off the cart and left dangling. Reg did a smart turn about and collected me. My mother, from our cottage opposite the rectory and churchyard, saw this and would not allow me to go on the cart again. I was allowed to go and muck the horses out and harness up, but no more trips.

Chapter 3

Living at the Village Inn

Like many thousands of women, my mother was lonely and a little afraid in the first years of the war, and for a time her youngest sister came to live with us – she was not many years older than me. She was a town girl, having been born in a small, busy Northamptonshire marketing town, and it showed in her dress and manner.

You will remember that our house overlooked the churchyard and we often had to walk through this, past some of the old gravestones, on our way home. What a golden opportunity for a country boy, who was used to the dark (I can't remember street lights for many years), to creep up behind Auntie Cis, scaring her so much that she would run home as fast as her legs could carry her. Her bedroom faced the church and on moonlit nights, I would get her to look out over the churchyard and would make all kinds of silly remarks – 'Look, that gravestone moved! Look at that grave,' (one with an uneven mound), 'that chap's got his knees up,' – taking all the confidence away from her.

One night when she was going to bed, holding the flickering candle high, she opened her bedroom door, gave an almighty shriek, dropped the candle and fled downstairs to

Mother, shouting, 'There's a ghost on the foot of my bed!' My mother tried to calm her whilst she found and lit another candle, all the time shouting for me to get up and see what all the fuss was about. I peeped through Cis's door, feeling quite scared myself, and sure enough, Cis was right, I could see a large white thing with big eyes. As Mother came up the twisty stairs with a new candle, this thing flew straight at my face. I grabbed it and hung on like grim death. Feathers flew everywhere and I was petrified. Mother came in with the light and found me clutching an old owl! How she laughed! We put it out of the window, for that's how it must have got in. Needless to say, I played no more tricks on Cis.

Not long after that, we were walking back from visiting an uncle and aunt on a very dark night, Cis and myself some distance in front of Mother, when we both saw a white object dancing on top of a gate. We raced back to mother and clung to her, shouting, 'There's a ghost on the gate, we've both seen it!' Mother pulled us forward until we could see this 'ghost' jumping up and down, sometimes quite high, and sometimes going from side to side.

'Stand still,' said Mother, 'the moon will break through any moment and you'll both be able to see your ghost better.'

In no time at all the moon broke through and there stood an old cart-horse with his head over the gate and with a large white blaze down his face. He had obviously heard us walking along the road and wanted a fuss making of him.

That was lesson number two for me. Young Aunt Cis went back home after her stay, not caring much for the country, but liking my baker friend Reg, and for some time to come.

Soon after this my father came home on leave and during this time the landlord of our village inn had his call-up papers. Conscription had started in earnest. My father and the landlord thought it might be to the advantage of both their wives if Mother and I went to live at the pub. The women would be company for one another, and running a public house was quite a responsibility for one person. My mother agreed to this as she liked Mrs Woodford, the landlady, and had had such a long time without adult company that she was not looking forward to another winter, with just we two.

So we moved in. I think the arrangements were that the work would be shared, also the housekeeping as far as the food went, and that an elderly man would tend to the barrels of beer and do the rough work. These arrangements must have worked well, because I noticed a definite change in my mother. She laughed more, and it was a pleasure to sit at the table with Mrs Woodford who laughed and joked as we ate our meals. As for me, I now had plenty of room to move about; long passages, a dark cellar to visit, where I inhaled the sweet smell of dripping beer, dipped my fingers in the drip trays and licked them – great fun! There were no pipes, and every pint sold had to be brought up from the cellar, which must have been a leg-aching job. Upstairs, I wandered along winding passages, looking first in one room, then another, running around in a large club room, where meetings were held, in order to hear my footsteps on the bare boards and spending ages in the billiard room. My instructions were, 'You can roll the balls by hand, but on no account must you use the cues.' I think they were afraid I would tear the cloth – little did they know that the young cat, little more than a kitten, would jump up on to the table and we would knock the balls to one another. The cat would leap in the air and pounce on fast running balls, killing them right, left and centre. We both enjoyed our game.

Outside the back door was a tall iron-handled water pump. If you turned the tap one way the water came out of the spout, and if you turned it the other way the pumping forced the water up to a tank in the roof. We had cold water taps over the sinks and, wonder of wonders, a toilet that flushed. One of my jobs was to pump the water up to the tank until it ran out from the overflow on the roof. The novelty of this task soon wore off, and I had to be bribed with a biscuit or two to get it done (always cream crackers). If I wanted to get away in a hurry I would agree to share my biscuits with a friend, and we would have the tank running over in no time at all.

In the yard of the pub there were stables and loose boxes, a tack-room with a bedroom above – no doubt used at one time – and coach-houses. In one of these was a gleaming monster of a car, which Mr Woodford had bought just before his call-up, to be used for hire, I believe. It was a Renault, with a dumpy, sloping bonnet, huge brass head-lamps, run on acetylene gas, and brass oil side-lamps which were fitted high up. There was a huge serpentine horn with a rubber bulb which you squeezed to make the most horrifying of sounds. I played for hours imagining I was driving this square-shaped, tall, solid old car with a luggage rack on the roof. I recall that coats of arms were painted on the doors – it must originally have belonged to nobility. I remember, years after the war, seeing this old car polished and bedecked with wedding ribbons; someone's proud possession.

Past the coach-house was a large vegetable garden which had a hen-run in one corner with about a dozen hens and a monster of a cockerel, beautifully marked but very spiteful indeed. When you collected the eggs, he would come for your legs, flying at you, spurs first. I was afraid of my face and eyes being injured, so I always took a long stick to ward him off, and I often knocked him over, but to no avail. I think he grew fiercer after these encounters, but at least I tried to show him who was boss. I think he had better luck with the women. Either Mother or Mrs Woodford, who I now called 'Aunt', would come in red-faced – 'Look what that cockerel has done – mud all over me,' or it could be, 'Look, he's torn my stockings. We'll have him for dinner one of these days.'

Sure enough, when next Mr Woodford came home on leave, he pulled the old cockerel's neck, and we *did* have him for dinner. I rather disgraced myself at the table: there was the cockerel on a dish, a monster of a bird, all golden and steaming; we all sat round the table and Mr Woodford, with great ceremony, stood over the bird, sharpening the carving knife, when he asked me, 'Where do you want a bit, boy?' and I, thinking of all the indignities I had suffered through that old bird, said, 'A bit off his arse!' shocking my mother, who felt ashamed of me, but sending Mr and Mrs Woodford into fits of laughter. For years afterwards I was not allowed to forget this, and whenever a knife was sharpened over a bird, someone or other would look at me and say, with a twinkle in his eye, 'Where do you want a bit, boy?' Nowadays, when we sit down to Christmas dinner at two tables pushed together, my wife, our children and seven grandchildren, I look at the youngest one, who was born on my birthday, and I feel he is not unlike me when I was his age. He has a happy face, is always first at the table and sits there with his knife and fork at the ready (no manners, says his mother); as I stand with knife poised over the turkey, I say, 'Where do you want a bit, Jake?' and I know that one day I shall get the answer I've been waiting for – 'A bit off his arse, Gramp!'

Living in a pub was quite good fun. In the early evenings I was allowed to sit in the bar and listen to my elders discussing the war, their work, and how their crops were turning out, but I was barred from the taproom. When I asked why, I was told, 'There are spitoons in there and the men spit into them and sometimes miss – not a place for a boy.' When I heard the laughter coming from the room, and heard the rattle of table skittles, I was quite envious and thought, 'Just the room for me, I know I can spit as good as the rest.' Even now, when I go to my little village pub, I choose the taproom in preference to the bar-lounge – so much more fun.

Bedtime in a pub is not so good for a child, you don't like leaving the company, and when you are tucked up in bed you hear the murmur of voices and bursts of laughter from the company downstairs and it's a job to get to sleep.

With two women to look after me, my life was not my own. I dodged and hid, but one or the other would catch me and introduce me to soap and water.

My greatest shame came one May Day. Together with other boys I was chosen to be one of the May Queen's retinue. We were asked to enter into the spirit of the occasion and dress for the part. What an excuse for two gifted needlewomen to meet the challenge! They cut and measured, treadled their old sewing machines (we still have my mother's machine – the drawers crammed with reels of cotton, buttons, hooks, thread, pins and tape – just as good as the day she bought it eighty years ago), and in no time at all I was fitted out with blue knee-breeches, with bows of ribbon at the knee, a tunic shirt and a large-brimmed hat with, to top it all, an ostrich feather, taken from one of the women's hats, and draped gracefully on mine – talk about Boy Blue!

At the dress rehearsal I found I was more or less in line with my mates, so this had a calming effect on me, and I really quite enjoyed the dancing and singing those lovely old May Day songs on the day. Dancing the maypole fascinated me; those intricate patterns woven by the dancing children were, I thought, very clever. (I still like to see it done.) After we had paraded the village, in order to collect more money we had to go to the outlying houses and farms, leaving the maypole behind, of course, the May Queen and her train-bearers leading the way with her attendants following. We sang and rattled the collection boxes and so on to another farm, another house, and this is where life became unbearable for me. The farm men, who I knew from their visits to the pub, passed all kinds of derogatory remarks about my appearance, and that was the straw that broke the camel's back. Off I ran with another boy, who was equally fed up, into the woods, and there we hid until going-home time; he was dressed in the same style as me and I'm sure that when the woodcocks, jays and other fine-feathered birds looked down at us, they thought what fine fellows we were.

Mrs Woodford's father, Mr Ross, was a farmer of the type you like to conjure up in your minds nowadays, when the hustle and bustle of modern living and ways seem to get on top of you. It's so nice to think back and remember when life moved on at a leisurely pace, with time to sit and think, and sometimes to just sit. He lived in the next village to ours, on a farm which, I think, belonged to the church and which had been farmed in the same way by generations of good yeomen farmers. Everything seemed so right, the barns so huge and well-timbered – surely these could never be filled up? – and the cowsheds, pig-sties, outhouses and stables were placed to shelter the yard from the winter storms.

One day, when I was going up the field with Mr Ross, it appeared to me that the only blot on the landscape was the thick mud in the gateways, and I asked Mr Ross, 'Why do you always build the gates where there is mud?' This query was met with hearty laughter, but no explanation was given to me. The farm men all got to hear about it and would pull my leg and ask, 'Where would you put them?' It was not until some years later, when I was running after the hounds and held a little-used gate open for the huntsmen that the penny dropped. When the last of the hunt was through, churning up the grass and spattering me with mud, I had my answer as to why gates are always put in muddy positions! How thick can you be?

I enjoyed going shepherding with Mr Ross – he seemed to have so much time as he pointed things out to me;

'Look, this is a track left by a badger; see, an old fox has been here – keep still and you will see its cubs come out. Those feathers are from a partridge,' etc. Then we would fetch the cows in for milking, and when we called, the cows would lift their heads up from grazing, as much as to say, 'Is that the time?' and would slowly amble down to the gate, stopping every now and then to take another mouthful of grass on the way. On odd occasions we had to fetch one that pretended she didn't know it was milking time, and would then walk faster than the rest, mooing as she led the way into the cowshed.

I am reminded of these leisurely times when my granddaughters come to stay. Although they live just outside suburbia, they are never happier than when they are in the country. They are horse mad, and I get no peace until I either take them riding or to their gran's old home in the next village, the farm now belonging to our nephew and niece, John and Rosemary. They love to help with the cows, and in no time at all their wellingtons and jeans are covered with mud and cow-muck. With wisps of hay sticking to them, they look like proper cowgirls. Then off will go the little cavalcade consisting of Rosemary, the girls and three dogs (one dog comes from a neighbouring farm every day when it's time to fetch the cows, why I do not know), to some fields on the hills on the outskirts of the village. They prop open the road gate, spread out into various fields, and down from the hilltops will come the cows, congregating at the road gate until they are all there, then out they come for the half-mile walk through the village. This is when the fun starts. Sixty or more cows fill the road from path to path, and more often than not, on the path. This is at a time when the factory and office workers are coming home from the towns, nearly always in a hurry. If the cows are walking towards them, all well and good, they just sit it out and the cows will pass sedately by, but if they are following the cows and hope to make their way through the herd, too bad! They blow their horns, rev up their engines, shout and hit the sides of their cars with the flats of their hands, but all to no avail. I look at the cows, the girls, Rosemary and the dogs, who are as calm and unhurried as Mr Ross was all those years ago, before the coming of the motor car, and, wicked me, I think 'Good on yer!'

Mr Ross's farmhouse was typical of good Northamptonshire craftsmanship, built of local stone with stone mullion windows and a thick, thatched roof. No fancy work, just plain and strong looking, the warm stone reminding you of the sunny days of summer, even in winter.

The house we now live in is built of the same stone and our grandchildren often stand examining it, finding all kinds of fossils embedded in it, and talking learnedly of how many million years old this one is and how many million years that one. Unlike Farmer Ross's house, ours had a new slate top put on in 1900, without, to my mind, upsetting the balance.

Twenty years or more ago, my wife was making enquiries about a porch over our back door, from the partner of an old established local building firm; we have used these builders for years – such splendid workmen – 'No hurry, we must have things right,' they would say. Alas, they are no longer in business, they grew old and could not keep up with the times.

'Fred,' said my wife, 'what about a porch here?'

'That's no problem,' said Fred, who was nearly eighty then, 'putting the top on these three cottages and making them into one house was the first job my father did as a firm. Before then, one family were stonemasons, another family carpenters, another painters and so on, and in 1900 they all got together and founded our firm.' He went on to say that all the cottages over the years were built by this family method. How well they have stood the ravages of time; our deeds go back to the Enclosure Act, and the cottages were not new then.

'Well,' my dear wife said, 'let's get back to this porch. I've been wanting one for years – how high will it be?' Whereupon Fred picked up a stone and threw it up the wall.

'It'll be as high as that stone,' he said.

'But the stone's come down,' said I, greatly amused at all this, and not wanting to shell out for a porch. 'Would you not rather measure?'

'No,' said Fred, 'I know how high that stone went.'

Nowadays, when I go to the DIY shop and come home with some nicely square kitchen unit top, which, when I go to fit it in a corner, fits only where it touches, I think, no wonder, if Fred's ancestors also threw stones to get the correct measurements inside the house too!

Mr Ross's farmhouse had a back porch that ran nearly all the way along one wall, and all manner of things were housed under its roof. Just against the door was a row of hooks upon which poultry was hung at times, after being killed. I used to help Mr Ross to catch these birds. 'You can get into the cub better than me, boy,' he would say. I have never seen anyone, with the exception of my father, kill poultry so humanely – the bird's head in one hand, feet in the other, no pulling or wringing of necks – just a little click and the job was done. 'See, no kicking and struggling, that's the way.' I must say that I never, ever tried my hand at this, even when I grew up.

I loved the farm kitchen; it was such a big room and so cosy, with everything going on in it, yet it was also a place in which to sit and rest. I never did see the parlour – I think that was kept for weddings and funerals. The dairy was a cold, damp place with stone slab benches upon which stood large, round, flat pans full of milk coated with thick cream. This was skimmed off by hand with a skimmer – you often see them in antique shops nowadays, a flat piece of metal riddled with small holes and with a wooden handle. This method left so much cream behind that skimmed milk was quite a good buy for the people who came with their milk cans, which were filled to the top for a halfpenny.

The Ross's had an elderly relative who lived in a little old cottage at the other end of the village. He lived the life of a recluse, but, nevertheless, another boy and myself were able to wheedle our way in, sit ourselves down on a stool and chair by the fireside and keep very quiet for some time. After a while we would say to the lonely old man, 'Tell us about when you were a soldier and fought for the Queen.' After a considerable pause, with much spitting on his part, he would start talking. I have never seen anyone to compare with his accuracy in spitting, directing a jet through his front teeth straight into the fire, very seldom touching a fire bar. How we envied him, and the times I have practised this art, but all to no avail. It would have been great to have jetted a stream of spit into his fire to show we were mates.

His yarns kept us spellbound. Which war he fought in, whether it was the Crimean or Boer war, I shall never know, and it did not matter to we boys. He told us how he had charged at full gallop, sword in hand, slashing here and slashing there, sending heads rolling off, and cutting off ears by the score. The battle tale we liked best was when one day he found himself far in front of his troop and going full tilt, sword in hand, at the Russian guns; his horse cleared the gun emplacement and there was a Russian soldier bending down to put another shell in his gun breach, and with one almighty slash of his sword, he cut off both cheeks of this Russian's backside! What a hero!

He took us to Africa and we clung to our seats as he told us how he out-rode and out-shot the Boers and the hundreds of miles he rode to take messages back for reinforcements, just him, his horse, and his water-bottle, getting there just in time to save the day. There is no doubt we were welcome company for this old man. As we sat there, enormous black beetles ran around our feet and in and out of the ashes that had spilled from the fire and had mounted up after several days. Soldier *par excellence*, yes! House-proud, no!

Of all the yarns he told us, none was ever malicious or mentioned real people, with the exception of the old Queen, God Bless Her! After some contemplation, either to get his wind or to make it more dramatic, I don't know which, he would say, 'Have I ever told you that I was the best skater in the regiment? Well, I was. I remember we were resting in Buckinghamshire and near our temporary barracks were some very large houses, with enormous lakes. The weather turned so cold and it froze and froze for days – one of the worst winters I can remember. When we had time on our hands, many of us went skating. How I used to win money off the officers by jumping over more wooden barrels than them! I remember I once jumped over six barrels pushed together. I had to take a long run to get up sufficient speed in order to do this.

'Well, one day I went further afield and found just the lake for skating on; the ice shone like glass, and although it was in front of a very large mansion, no one was on it. I sat on the bank, put on my skates, and off I went like the wind, first on one leg, then the other, twisting and turning and making figures of eight. I was lost to the world. Then I heard voices, and looking up, saw a party of gentlefolk on the bank. I skated on but kept well away from them, hoping I would not get into trouble. Then I saw a gentleman detach himself from the group and come towards me. When we were within speaking distance, he said, "I say, what's your name?" "Corporal Jim Ross, Sir," I said. "Well, Corporal Jim Ross, the Queen would like a word with you."

'My heart stood still. I skated over to Her Majesty and drew myself to attention, straight as a ram-rod, not daring to look at her. "Jim Ross," said Her Majesty, "I haven't seen such skating for years. It would give me pleasure if you would partner me on the ice." "Yes, Ma'am," I stammered.

'I held out my hands and helped Her Majesty on to the ice, noticing many a stern look from the attendant gentlemen. We crossed our hands, as skaters do, and off we went in step. I was frightened to death in case she should fall, but

I soon discovered that she was a better skater than me. "Come along, Jim," Her Majesty said, "let's go fast, and then we will do a waltz."

'We must have looked unusual, a young corporal waltzing with his Queen on ice! I thought, I'll never tell any of my mess mates about this, and I never did. After all these years have passed, you boys are the first I have ever told.'

How privileged we were. I could never understand, when I repeated this tale to my mother and Mrs Woodford, why they would clap their hands to their mouths, go red in the face, bolt from the room with tears in their eyes, and I would hear shrieks coming from along the passage.

In 1937, when my wife and I were married, Mr and Mrs Woodford came to the wedding reception. I asked about old Jim, only to be told he had fought and lost his last campaign quite a few years ago. I expected this reply, but still felt sad. It often crosses my mind nowadays that with men like old Jim, no wonder we ruled a quarter of the globe.

Chapter 4

The War to End All Wars

I do not seem to have said very much about the dreadful war that was being waged. As a boy, I was very conscious of the titanic struggle that was going on, but France, in those days of slow travel, did seem a long way away, so unlike the Second World War, with the Blitz going on all around us, the blackout, the crump of bombs, the fires lighting up the night sky, the German planes droning overhead almost every night, and in the case of Coventry, all night. You felt as if you were in the front line.

During the First World War, communication for the people was more or less non-existent. No wireless, very few private telephones, and newspapers were not read by all. If you lived in a small village in the heart of the country, say ten miles from the nearest town, with no army camps in the vicinity, everything about the war seemed so vague and unreal. Not so for the wives, mothers and sweethearts of the young men who had volunteered to fight. We would see them go and then in a few weeks they would come back in their uniforms, looking so smart with their boots shone up, putties neatly wound, trousers creased and buttons and cap badges glistening. We felt so proud of them; then one day we would see them with bayonets at their sides, kitbags packed, canvas webbing, water-bottles – the lot – and rifles slung over their shoulders. We knew they were going overseas, and so did their poor womenfolk, and down to the station we would go to see them off.

The station signal-boxes were our contact with the outside world; messages would come tick, tick, ticking over on a machine and the railway men would tell us what was said. We began to hear of dreadful battles and of U-boats sinking our shipping. These few and far-between reports we chose not to believe. I had a rude awakening when my father came home on leave after about eighteen months overseas. He hardly recognised me, I had grown so, and I was not too sure of him until I saw him turn into our house.

I can remember his clothes being lousy and I can see my mother now, attacking all the seams of his shirt, vest and pants with a hot iron, whilst Dad lay in bed. I would look at the little grey-coloured beasts creeping about and call to Mother, 'Here's some! Here's some more!' – shouting with glee at the sound of the popping under the hot iron. But I felt very sad when I looked at my mother's face, and saw that she was quietly weeping. What a shock it must have been to those mothers and wives, in a period of time when cleanliness was next to Godliness, seeing their loved ones in such a sorry state, and thinking of them having to put up with such conditions for weeks on end. I remember being told by one old soldier, 'We hung our shirts up in the frosty weather, hoping the frost would kill them,' or, 'We turned our shirts inside out, giving the little beggars a day's march, before they could get us again.' Then again, I've heard it said, 'When we came out of the trenches on rest, we would be fumigated, have a bath and be issued with clean underwear. These had belonged to the regiment which had been through before us. You just hoped you had not followed the Guards, or your shirts would fit where they touched!'

When we made the journey to my grandfather's, to enable my mother to see her brothers and brothers-in-law who were home on leave, they too had experienced the same conditions if they had been in the trenches. One of them was in the Navy, and he seemed to fare much better – 'We take our home about with us,' he chuckled, 'all ship-shape and Bristol fashion.' This sailor uncle lost a leg in one of the Naval battles and, after months and months in hospital, was invalided out of the Navy on a small pension. I hung on every word that was said to my grandfather – I heard words like U-boats, and Scapa Flow, Mons and Ypres (Wipers to the Tommies). Then my grandfather said, 'They have brought in conscription so you will soon get some help.' I understand that by 1916, when conscription was introduced, two and a half million men had volunteered – Britain's wonderful Volunteer Army.

To the front of my grandfather's house was a large field which undulated – I rather think that at some time it had been mined for stone or iron-ore – but was now completely grassed over. It was an ideal adventure playground for children and I would join the town boys there and have great fun. Imagine my surprise when next I went to stay with Grandfather and found that this field had been completely transformed. It was covered with trenches which were occupied by hundreds of soldiers having mock battles, and on a word of command jumping out with fixed bayonets to charge some dummy men made of sacking, stuffed with straw, all the time emitting such blood-curdling shrieks. As they thrust their bayonets into the dummies, a corporal would shout, 'In – out! In – out!' all very exciting. There would be squads of other men drilling and all kinds of military activity was going on. My mother had a job to get me in the house for my dinner, so enthralled had I become.

When it was time for the soldiers to return to barracks, they would fall in and march smartly off, singing or whistling songs, such as 'It's a long way to Tipperary', and 'Pack up your troubles in your old kitbag', etc. The song which pleased we boys the most because of the swear words, went like this:

> We are Fred Karno's army,
> The ragtime infantry.
> We cannot fight, we cannot shoot,
> What bleeding use are we?
> And when we get to Berlin
> The Kaiser he will say,
> 'Hoch! Hoch! Mein Gott!
> What a bloody rotten lot!
> What a bloody rotten lot are they!'

Of course, sometimes other words were used – I think it depended on the mood of the soldiers!

Whilst I stayed at my grandfather's I saw my first Zeppelin. This was caught in the beams of some search-lights and looked to me like a huge silver fish. It was during an air raid, the only raid I can remember. I was awakened by my mother to the wailing of sirens and was pushed under the table to join my frightened aunts. What with the sirens, the gunfire, and the trembling aunts saying their prayers, I burst into tears. My grandfather said, 'Give the boy to me and don't panic so – keep still, if we go up we will go up together!' He sat in his chair holding me tightly on his lap when we heard an almighty bang. I looked over his shoulder out of the window, and that's when I saw the Zeppelin. The next day I went with Grandfather to feed the pigs on his allotment, and there, some way behind the sty, was a bomb crater. We had no idea it was so close to home – a few more hundred yards and it would have hit the railway marshalling yards – not bad aiming for those days. I had something to tell my friends when I went back home to my quiet village.

The war dragged on and more and more men were called up to serve their country, some of them quite elderly. I am not sure, but I think the age group for conscription was eighteen to forty years old, extended towards the end of the war to forty-five years of age. Many years after the war, about 1933, my father-in-law-to-be would tell us, with many a chuckle, about when he had his call-up papers. Now my wife's father was a quiet, calm, scholarly man, and the most war-like gesture I have ever seen him make was to raise one eyebrow. We all respected him so much that that was sufficient to quell any unseemly or boisterous horseplay. Father-in-law explained:

'I caught the train to Towcester and found the Ministry examination room where I gave my name and age – forty-five. "Right," I was told, "go in there and strip out."

'Whilst I was being given my check over, one of the doctors asked me if I was married. Yes, I said. "Any children?"

Yes, I replied. "How many?" Ten and a half, I said, my three oldest boys are at the front. "My word," the examining-board said, "you're more use to us at home than you would ever be at the front!" '

He told this tale many times to the amusement of us all.

The women at home worked so hard doing mens' jobs, an unheard of thing in those days. Girls came from the towns and cities to work on the land and tend the stock as well as milking, threshing, harvesting and ploughing etc. No task was too hard or too dirty. They joined the Women's Voluntary Service and the Red Cross, they sewed, knitted and beavered away; they drove buses and cars in the towns, worked on the railway and in factories and joined the Services in their hundreds. A new freedom for women was born – never again would they be totally housebound.

A lot more people went to church than they do today. It was expected of me to go with Mother every Sunday. I can remember now sitting next to her, squeezing close to keep warm, putting one hand in her muff to warm my fingers, and being told not to put my feet on the hassock, as they were for kneeling on. I would close one eye and make different shapes and patterns with the beautiful coloured rays that came through the windows, or look for a bird that had found its way into the church, follow its flight and secretly hope it would land on the rector!

These daydreams were shattered during one Sunday morning service when we all heard the door open and the sound of nailed boots on the flagstone floor. Down the aisle came a village youth, looking very important. 'Rector,' he shouted, 'the rectory is on fire!' The rector made suitable excuses and left us in the charge of one of the church wardens. How I wished the church warden would hurry up and let us out – I wanted to see all that was going on at the rectory. When at last we were allowed out, the fire was under control. It was caused by a chimney catching fire, I was told, and afterwards, in the pub, I heard a customer say, 'I bet that's the only time that old rectory's ever been warm.'

During those war years we had some Belgian refugees living in the village. I think the father of one of the families must have had an important war job as he had a car, and what a funny car it was – a little two-seater open to the skies with a dickey seat at the back. But the odd part about it, in my opinion, was that there was no steering wheel! In place of a wheel it had a bar. I now know that this was described as tiller steering. Two Belgian boys were showing us round this little car and they climbed in and sat in the driver's seat. We jumped up and down on the running-boards, but unfortunately the brake could not have been left on properly, and it was most important that it should have been, because the car had been left at the top of a steep, narrow lane. Away careered the car backwards, down the lane, across a road, and the rear portion crashed through a cottage window! A great shock for the family inside the cottage, no doubt! Thankfully no one was hurt, although I'm not too sure about the two Belgian boys when confronted by their irate father!

About a month before the end of the war, my mother's favourite brother, Jack, was killed. He was in the Bedfordshire Regiment and had been in action from the beginning of hostilities. To go through all those battles over the years, and to endure such terrible hardships, then just when you think the end of the war is in sight, to be killed, seems particularly cruel. My mother and I went to see my grandparents – at these sad times it's a comfort to have your family around you.

My grandmother was very upset over the loss of her eldest son, but I couldn't make out how his loss had affected my grandfather. He was very quiet and sat in his chair in the living-room hardly speaking. I was told not to bother him and to play in the garden as much as possible.

One day two men came to the door, knocked and were admitted. Being nosey, I went indoors just in time to see my mother ushering them into the living-room.

'Dad,' she said, 'someone to see you.'

I hung about in the kitchen, trying to hear what was said, and I heard my gramp's voice raised which was most unusual, then, with a crash, the dividing door burst open. Now, I have told you what a huge man my grandfather was – he had one of the callers by the throat, whilst shouting at me to open the back door, and he slung him out. The other man was protesting and my grandfather grabbed him by the scruff of his neck and pushed him out of the door, kicking his backside as he did so. My grandfather swore, the first and only time I heard him blaspheme, and shouting, 'Don't you come back here again with your blood money,' went back into his room.

My mother and Granny looked amazed, and Granny said that in all her married life she had never seen him like that before, and neither had I. When things had calmed down in the kitchen the gas cooker needed straightening as one of the men, in his hurry to get out, had collided with it.

I wanted to know what blood money was, and £25 was mentioned. It was for poor Uncle Jack, I was told. It's such a long time ago, I cannot remember too clearly; could it have been an insurance that Uncle Jack had taken out when he worked as a butcher before the war which Gramp had kept paid up for him, or could it have been help from the Government, the going rate for the loss of a son? I don't know, but I do know that Grandfather would not touch it and never did.

Years afterwards, we moved to the village I still live in. My father was still in the Police Force and it was one of several moves he was forced to make during his service years – a bit off-putting when you had got to know everyone, but I suppose these moves were necessary. One day, mother came in from shopping in this new village, very excited. She said, 'Who do you think I've just seen? Old Sergeant Haynes, who was my father's driver when father was a superintendent!' She went on to say that she remembered him from when she was a girl. Apparently he had lived in the village in retirement for years. When I had some time to spare, I called on Sergeant Haynes and his wife. What a grand old gentleman he was. After I got to know him better, we would sit by his fire and he would tell me of the days when he and Grandfather were together in lots of rowdy situations. Granny may not have seen Gramp 'like that before', but my goodness, Sergeant Haynes had! I'll try and remember to tell you more later on.

The war by now had seemed to envelop the whole world. Events on the home front had reached fever pitch. I heard grown-ups saying, 'The end is in sight; it can't go on much longer – one more push by our men and it will be all over.' The word 'armistice' was mentioned, and before long indeed, the war was over.

There was great rejoicing, with people in the streets shouting, 'It's over! We've won! Our boys will be coming home now.' Flags were hung from windows, church bells rang unceasingly in celebration. What a relief for mothers and wives whose loved ones were prisoners of war, and what a relief for those whose husbands and sons had come safely through the horrors of the fighting. The parish council and local dignitaries got together and arranged victory celebrations for the whole village. For some reason or other, apart from remembering seeing the village flag bedecked, I can't recall any of the festivities – a funny thing, that, there must be a mental blockage somewhere.

I do remember my father coming home for good about twelve months after the cessation of hostilities. He had been with the army of occupation and for some time was billeted in the home of a German police sergeant, who had been fighting for his country and was now back in the German police force. They must have had a lot to talk about. It was the same for others in the forces; it was many a month before they were demobilised.

In the late 1920s I remember thinking, as I looked about me and saw those brave men who had fought so gallantly for their King and Country, nearly all of them unemployed, many so badly injured that they were unable to work, some poor chaps coughing up their lungs from the effects of poison gas, the same picture repeated wherever you went, market town, county town or city, did we really win the war? Can anyone win in war? These were the lucky ones, but what about those that were killed? What would they have achieved had they lived? What inventions would they have created? Maybe something outstanding and revolutionary which would have got us out of this mess. What doctors, scientists, sportsmen, explorers etc., were cut down in their youth? My word, I thought, what dreadful distress can be caused to the people of the world by their leaders and politicians, nearly all of them old men, in the name of patriotism.

But at least, we were told, it was not all in vain – this was the war to end all wars – well, until 1939!!

Chapter 5

Post-War and Beginning to Relax

After the armistice was signed, much to everyone's relief, things went on very much the same in our village. In a purely agricultural area, life is governed by the seasons. You must plough, sow, hoe and harvest, in that order, what ever happens to the world about you. Stock must be unceasingly tended and you so seldom heard any of the land workers complain about their annual allotted tasks. You could, if you liked to listen to them, hear their bosses, the farmers, moan and groan about losing money, saying that they could not afford this, and they couldn't afford that, but no true country man takes any notice of them, they just smile at these tales of woe which they have heard all their lives. Indeed, you only have to look at a farmer's waistcoat, with the buttons straining, and compare him with his workers who, even if they are bent with age, are still as slim as in their youth, to realise who is unable to afford this and unable to afford that. I have known many an old farm labourer to have only one suit all his life, and this was the suit he was married in. It may have turned green with age, but, my goodness, he could still do it up. I often think what good material those suits must have been made from, taking into account a farm labourer's pay. They couldn't have been very expensive, even when bought new. The suits would be brought out of the upstairs cupboards for wear on Sundays and bank holidays, village fêtes, pig-club outings, Odd Fellows and Foresters' days out. Everyone would look quite smart, always with flowers in their buttonholes, a gay-coloured neckerchief, and hobnailed working boots, blacked and polished.

The suits were worn with a more sombre neckerchief when the wearers carried the coffins of their friends and loved ones shoulder high to their last resting place. If the distance was too great to the churchyard, the parish bier was used. It always seems to me to be so much more fitting on these sad occasions, and so much more dignified, to be taken to your last resting place pushed or carried by friends, rather than in a shiny cavalcade of glistening motors, driven by people hurrying to get the job done and on to the next one. Perhaps the modern way is best for the family mourners, I don't know, and I mustn't go on so.

I did notice that, at times, those old villagers wore different items in their buttonholes, perhaps a piece of ivy, or something similar, to show that they belonged to the same Friendly Society – all very mysterious and simple.

As I was saying, after the armistice not much change was noticed in the working day, but there was a remarkable change in the village itself. People were much more relaxed and before long, plans were being made for the Christmas festivities. The Christmases over the last few years had been rather austere, due to shortages. Although the men were not yet home from the forces, everyone felt that they could bring out of storage the things they had been so carefully hoarding and celebrate a Christmas that the children would remember for a long time to come.

I can still remember my amazement when I was told that Father Christmas had been and left my presents in the billiard room on the billiard table. Although I had my doubts about there being a Father Christmas, I raced upstairs to find the billiard room table literally covered with presents from my mother, Mrs Woodford, my grandparents and a host of aunts. Not very big and expensive items but lots and lots of colourful toys and books. I remember one book cost two shillings and sixpence, a small fortune then, and there was a parcel sent by my father from Germany for my mother and me. When we undid it, so much of the contents had been broken or bent in transit it was a shame.

Just before Christmas, some workmen put two telephone wires up which were fastened to our house and went on to the post office. I used to imagine, when the cold east winds blew through the wires and made them hum, that it was an aeroplane with Father Christmas on board and thought how lovely it would be if he dropped toys down the chimney. No such luck! I soon learned that when the wires moaned and vibrated, making a humming noise, snow was on the way. Today, when I hear the same sound, I say, 'that's a snow wind,' and it usually is.

After Christmas, when the nights began to draw out and daylight lasted a little longer, we boys would play my favourite game, Fox and Hounds. Village boys usually go about in gangs, and what better game for a gang to play than Fox and Hounds? Remember, we had no street lights so the dark, frosty, star-lit nights – sometimes with a little moonlight – were ideal. We would send two boys off to be the foxes, count up to one hundred, then shout that we were ready and were coming to find them. Off we would go in a pack, stopping every now and then to listen for the 'foxes'. There would be no sound in the village other than that made by we boys. If we could not hear them we would shout 'Holler, else the little puppy dogs can't follow!' You would then hear a faint imitation of an old dog fox barking, and off we would go full pelt to catch them, but invariably those two foxes had moved on to a different hiding place. 'Holler,' we would cry again, and so it went of for hours, until we either caught them or they gave up, when we would break up and go home to bed.

I can remember to this day, opening the door to our house, smelling the paraffin oil-lamp fumes, and seeing the blazing fire, with the kettle singing on the hob. Mother, seeing my face aglow would say, 'You've had a lovely time – those old foxes have led you a dance tonight. I heard you go past here several times – I should think you will sleep well tonight,' and so I did. It was so perfectly safe in those days to roam the streets, the fields and go just where your fancy took you. There were no motor cars to interrupt the games and they were all played in the streets.

There were different seasons for different games – on one day not a whip and top in sight and on the next day, for some inexplicable reason, everyone was wielding them. And so it was with all the games, out would come the bags of marbles, blacksmith-made iron hoops were brought out of sheds – the girls would have wooden ones – then shiny conkers appeared threaded on strings, when each player would try to break that held by his opponent. There was one dangerous game called tip-tap when you took a piece of round wood, sharpened at both ends to a point, rested it on a brick with a point overlapping, then struck the end of the pointed wood with a good, sturdy stick. When it flew up in the air you gave it an almighty swipe with your stick, knocking it as far as possible. This tapping and hitting was repeated three times, and the person who knocked the tip the farthest with three taps, won the game. I was very fond of this chancy game. When I say chancy, I mean for eyes and windows. Five-stones was a summer game and we would sit for hours in the sun, girls and boys, engrossed in the game. Rounders was also played in the road with complete safety.

Thinking about the safety of the roads for children in my youth, reminds me of an old lady in our village who used to be on the look-out for me. She would be leaning on the door jamb of her house when it was time for me to go by. 'Come here, my duck,' she would call (every child was called 'my duck' in that part of Northamptonshire), 'I want you to run an errand for me to – (she would mention the name of the next village). I'll give you a slice of cake.'

Thinking of the four miles I had to walk, when I could be enjoying myself with my friends, I must have pulled a face, showing I did not relish running this errand. 'Come on, my duck,' the old lady repeated, 'You see, my legs hurt me so much or I would go.'

'Yes, but the slice of cake you gave me last week was so dry, I had a job to eat it,' was my reply.

'Don't worry my duck,' she said, 'I'll put some jam on it this time.' How could I refuse her? For ages afterwards

I ran or walked my four miles a week for a slice of cake, but always now with jam on it.

One country custom I enjoyed was gleaning. It was like a day out for we children and maybe also for our mothers. We took our tea baskets to the harvest field and waited for the last sheaf of corn to be picked up and put on the wagon. This was the signal for us to go into the field and pick up all the loose corn that the binder had missed. Everyone recognised that if a farmer did not want, or was not ready for you to glean, he left one sheaf upright in the field, and that meant no gleaning. Once the all-clear was given, we all trooped in, laughing and talking, and after spreading ourselves out, would start gleaning. The ladies wore large aprons tied round their waists which were held up with one hand, leaving the other hand free, and into these would go the long straws of corn with the ears pointing all one way. In no time at all the aprons would be full of corn which would be heaped in selected spots, each family keeping to their own heap with the children adding their bundles to the growing piles. People with large families came out best, of course.

After a time our arms became red and sore with the chafing of the sharp wheat straw, and we young ones would begin to flag and start to play around. The womenfolk would take the hint and call out 'Tea-time', when we all gathered in a circle, and with lots of laughing and a bit of leg-pulling, would eat our food and drink cold tea out of bottles. When the food had disappeared, the women would settle down for a rest, telling we children not to go too far away. Indeed, they had earned their rest, for gleaning is a back-breaking job – you are bent double for most of the time. We were glad of the opportunity to do as we liked, and the boys would scour the hedgerows for birds' nests while the girls would either pick wild flowers or make plaited corn-dollies – some of the bigger ones were quite expert at this. Before long we would be called upon to start work. This we did, not quite as enthusiastically as when we had started the day, but it was very noticeable how the heaps had grown.

After the menfolk had finished work, they came to the field with their hand-trucks and barrows, tied the corn in bundles and lashed the whole lot on them, then off home the tired and dusty gleaners would go. Some families would gather so much over the season they would ask the threshing box men to put it through the drum after they had finished the farmer's threshing. The boltings of straw would be taken home for the pig-sty bedding and the corn taken to the mill. I think the miller kept a percentage of the resulting flour for payment but this was more likely to happen with men who had also grown corn on their allotments. Most families had large allotments which they worked to help keep them through the winter months. Half an acre was not unusual. I remember one old man who had so much ground he kept a donkey to help him work it, complete with plough, hoe and donkey cart. He and his whole family were known as Donkey ★ ★ ★ ★ ★. No offence was meant and none was taken.

A life-long friend and workmate tells the tale of one very industrious allotment holder who sold some of his potatoes to a rather upmarket newcomer to the village for five shillings a cwt. Charlie, the allotment holder, said to my friend Dick, 'I say, Dick, if I had known that new chap wasn't going to pay for those potatoes I would've charged him double!'

I can remember allotment holders forming an association and working together, helping one another in all manner of ways, even hiring a threshing box to thresh their corn. This must have been very successful because I have seen wooden barrels of flour, times without number, just inside their back doors. Why they were kept inside the back door, I don't know. Was it to keep them cool, or was it a sign to say they were not hard up? I can't answer. The people with the smaller amount of gleaning, like my mother, laid the straw on the ground, beat the ears with a stick until all the corn had come out, then threw this into the air, letting the chaff blow away, so leaving the corn reasonably clean. This we stored and fed a little to the hens at a time; the straw was put into the nest boxes and on the floor of the hen-house and the hens would scratch about in it for days on end.

By now, with the war having been over for nearly a year, the village people had more leisure time, and with winter on the horizon, a village football team was formed. We had great pride in our team and woe-betide them if they lost! If at any time this looked likely, the pitch would be invaded by a tall, middle-aged lady, armed with an umbrella, who would lay about members of the visiting team should they dare show signs of winning or even hurt one of our lads in the rough and tumble of the game. She was a fearsome old lady and we were glad she was on our side – I think she was called Black Bess. What a rough lot we were!

The school team was no better. The only match I can remember playing in was against a bigger village than ours, situated two miles away. There was great rivalry between our two villages, mainly, I think, because they were more advanced than we were. We turned out determined to do as well as our senior team – we couldn't let the village down. It didn't matter too much about the school, none of us was too keen on school, but the visiting team had other ideas and in no time at all we were five or six goals down. Where was Black Bess? She had deserted, us so we had to take unusual measures ourselves. We attacked them, drove them off the field, out of the village and down the hill towards their own village. We pelted them all the way with sharp granite stones taken from heaps conveniently piled by the side of the road in readiness for future road repairs. The stones would be watered and squashed into the holes in the road by steamroller – no tar was used then to bind them together.

When we visited our ninety-four-year-old uncle, who witnessed the rout of our young neighbours, he sometimes recalled it, and when I said how glad I was that we didn't hurt anyone seriously with those sharp stones, he would say, 'I saw some of you throwing hoss muck at them – you couldn't do much damage with hoss muck!' I had no answer to this. He used to go on to tell the younger ones of our family about the tough fight he had, involving so many people. The main contestants were Uncle and the village roughneck. Apparently there had been a parliamentary election meeting at the working men's club. During the meeting things got a bit hectic, and tempers were getting frayed, with everyone trying to speak at once.

This heated meeting eventually came to an end, the people filed outside and stood, still arguing, in groups. The village roughneck was shouting at the top of his voice and expressing his opinion in no uncertain terms. Uncle, who was of a different political persuasion, called the chap's name and said, 'You talk like a fool!'

That was the spark that lit the fuse, and in no time at all, fists were raised, blows were struck and a general mêlée ensued. Uncle and his boisterous opponent got to grips in earnest – they went at it hammer and tongs. Eventually Uncle managed to get his opponent's head under his arm and held it there, thumping the man's face unceasingly with his other hand, until he cried for mercy – 'I've had enough,' he gasped, and someone in the crowd said, 'He's been asking for that for years.'

Uncle told us that he called at a friend's house to remove all traces of blood and to tidy up before going home as he didn't want to scare his wife, my aunt. On arriving home he opened the door and she said, 'What *have* you been up to! Millie Sykes has been here – she opened the door and threw a cap in, covered with blood, and said, "Here's your old man's cap, he's had a good hiding tonight and it serves him right!" ' Beatrice told her it wasn't her husband's cap as he didn't wear one and said, 'I bet that's the other chap's cap,' and so it was.

When we called to see Uncle not long before he died, I asked him how he was and he replied, 'Not too good, boy. I can't get going somehow.' He was soon to be ninety-five and I should have liked him to make one hundred. I wondered what I could say to buck him up, and it came to me in a flash.

'Do you remember that fight you had when you tucked that man's head under your arm?'

'My goodness, boy,' he said – he still calls me 'boy' although I'm a grey-haired old grandfather – 'My goodness, boy, I taught him a lesson.' Once again he relived the fight of sixty-five years ago, the man's head was captured under his arm, and he thumped away. The colour came back to his cheeks and he began to smile. That's more like your old self, I thought.

Before we left for home, a good samaritan of a neighbour made one of her several daily calls. Looking at Uncle she said, 'My word, their visit has done you good – you were quite poorly this morning, you couldn't eat and now look at you!' It would seem that if you can stir the blood with age-old fights, it is of considerable help as you battle on in later years. Maybe this is why generals and politicians reach such a ripe old age.

This same uncle would have been about twenty-three years of age at the outbreak of the 1914–1918 war, and as he was a very skilled and highly trained engineer he could undertake all sorts of engineering; in other words, he was a very gifted man, as later years were to prove. He was drafted to Rolls Royce in Derby for highly confidential war work. His wife, who was also a meticulous worker and skilled in so many ways, joined him in Derby and did important war work too. I did not see much of them until after the war, when they were released from their war work in Derby.

It would appear that Uncle had no wish to rejoin his old firm, so he decided to start a garage repair shop in a large shed in the inn yard in our village. Motor cars had begun to get more plentiful, farmers and tradesmen, apart from the gentry, were the proud owners of this new form of transport. Model T Fords were the most popular type chosen by the farmers in our area. I never liked the honking, smelly things, and I liked them far less when, at the age of fourteen, I drove them on the road. What vicious contraptions they were, you had to start them by hand and at the least provocation when the handle was swung they kicked back, skinning your knuckles or worse. Many people had their arms broken by a kick-back. If the weather was bitterly cold, to make starting easier you jacked up the rear wheel and this lessened the drag on the transmission, making it less difficult to turn the engine over. There was no gear box as such – the drive was transferred to the rear wheels by means of friction bands on a flywheel drum. There were three foot pedals, but unlike the modern car the centre one was not an accelerator, it was reverse gear. Once you had started the engine you released the handbrake half-way – that was neutral – pushed your left foot pedal progressively down and you were now in low gear. When your speed was right you pushed your handbrake right forward, and that was top gear. So your handbrake right off was top gear, pulled up half-way was neutral gear, and by pulling it farther you applied the handbrake. The right-hand foot pedal was the footbrake – all very simple; the accelerator was a hand lever on the steering wheel held in different positions by notches, and the other hand lever was the advance and retard of the magneto. Once you got going, a slight adjustment of the throttle lever was sufficient until you came to a hill.

I remember my uncle had been repairing the carrier's van.

It was a square box van with doors at the rear, and a long, folding seat on each side for the use of passengers. When there weren't passengers the seats were clipped up to make room for parcels. There was also a parcel rack on the roof to carry more goods, but for the driver and front-seat passenger there were no doors – the sides were quite open, with just a divided windscreen. There were no windscreen wipers, and if visibility became too bad, you opened the windscreen a little way and peered through the crack. It was more or less the design of a carrier's cart without the horse – pretty spartan travel.

Back to Uncle and his repairs. 'Come on Charlie,' he said to the owner, 'jump in and take her up to the turnpike.' Charlie sat behind the wheel, I got in the middle and Uncle was seated on my left. When we reached the turnpike, Uncle said, 'Give her full throttle, Charlie, try her out. I bet the old girl's never gone as well as this before.' Along we went at full speed, Charlie having nothing to do with his hands or feet, with the exception of steering straight, when, to my amazement, he disappeared without a word over the side of the van and out of sight. There we were, bowling along at full throttle, with no one at the wheel. (I was much too young then to be able to drive.) Uncle clambered over me, grabbed the steering wheel and slowed down as soon as possible, looking over the side of the van for Charlie.

'My God, I can't see him on the road – he must have gone under the wheels – he will be killed!' said Uncle.

I felt very apprehensive, wondering what we would find when we eventually stopped, but to my astonishment, into my side of the van clambered Charlie.

'Where the hell have you been?' shouted Uncle.

'I thought I heard a rattle at the back, so I got out to have a listen,' Charlie replied.

'You might have told us what you were going to do,' Uncle said, looking very cross, 'we could have been in the ditch, or worse.'

Charlie, as calm as you like, answered, 'I knew you would be able to take over.'

I smile to myself when I go along the Northampton turnpike today, and wonder what my chances would be, with present-day traffic, if I suddenly opened the driver's door, clambered along the side of the car, around the back and into the passenger's door – all this done at full throttle. Would my wife take over and save the day? Good old Charlie! Needless to say, with customers like Charlie, Uncle made very little profit, and in the end joined his brother in a gold and silversmith's business; much more fitting for his numerous and outstanding skills.

Chapter 6

The Great Day Arrives:
Father Comes Home for Good

There was great excitement at the inn. Mr Woodford was expected to arrive home any day soon, and my father would not be long after him, getting his discharge and finishing with the army after all those years. Mother started giving our police cottage a good spring clean, washing curtains, making up the beds, having the chimney swept, and polishing, dusting and scrubbing – not necessarily in that order. I suppose you could liken it to a bride getting a house ready for her new husband.

When Mr Woodford arrived at the station he was met by his wife and when they arrived at the pub was welcomed with resounding cheers by the customers. After dumping his kit and giving Mother and me a squeeze, he said, 'Now for a real pint,' and I feel sure it didn't stop at one, so pleased was he to be home. Mother and I went back to our own cottage, but Mother returned to the pub in the day time to enable Mr and Mrs Woodford to have some time off.

I discovered that Mr Woodford, who was never very robust, was in the medical corps and had been driving ambulances at the front. He never talked about his experiences to me, 'I want to forget,' he would say. I think he felt that things had been too dreadful to relate to young ears.

What a difference he made to the running of the pub. Everything seemed to run so smoothly and I'm sure the women breathed sighs of relief.

He was very keen on field sports and was often out with his gun and rod. The old retriever began to thin down and get into some kind of shape, but I think the years had told on her, because I heard Mr Woodford say, 'I shall have to get a young pup to help you out, old girl.' A young dog did arrive one day, but after several days out with him I overheard Mr Woodford telling his wife, 'He's not a patch on the old dog, but he'll learn.'

The great day arrived at last and my father came home. I was thrilled to see him, but it did seem strange to have a man in the house. I did not feel completely at ease, and I am sure that after being a sergeant major for so long and having to control men in no uncertain way, he found it difficult to deal with a boy. I really think we were shy of one another. Before Dad resumed his police duties we had a long holiday at his sister's house. My aunt Ada and Uncle Harry kept a small village inn and had a considerable sized smallholding, complete with all kinds of animals, bees and poultry of every hue and size – huge black and white speckledy hens, some with feathery legs, and hosts of bantams of all sizes; some were supposed to have their feathers growing backwards, but I could never see this, they just looked a bit windswept to me.

On the other side of the smallholding, my Uncle Harry, who was a sign-writer by trade, as was his father before him, had had a workshop built, complete with several sheds and a super stable, in which was kept a high-stepping horse.

A very smart trap was housed in one of the sheds and this was his pride and joy. He had painted and varnished it numerous times and then, with his sign-writing brushes, had trimmed it with gold and black lines everywhere, down all the wheel spokes, the wheel hubs, the fellies where the rubber tyres fitted, along the shafts and the trap body. The whole turn-out glistened and gleamed. This, no doubt, was an advertisement for him, for one of his jobs he did in his workshop was to paint and sign-write traps and tradesmen's vans. The larger farm wagons he painted at the local wagon-builder's yard.

It was so interesting to see the skill of the wagon builders, making those huge wagon wheels, starting with the solid hubs. These were turned out on a primitive lathe, treadled by foot to get the lathe turning, then the operator would hold various shaped chisel-like tools against the spinning block of wood and you could see the hub beginning to take shape. It was then finished by hand with all the square holes chiselled out for the spokes to be fitted. These were cut from well-seasoned wood, sawn square, then shaped and fitted into the hub. The fellies would be cut next and fitted to the spokes and, as if by magic, you had a giant wagon wheel, minus the solid, thick iron tyre, which was made and fitted by the village blacksmith. This was a hot and sweaty job, and I can picture the men now, with their roaring fire outside the forge, heating this huge, heavy iron ring, which had been made previously in the forge, and the wooden wheel laying on its side on a flat, iron platform. When the moment was right the blacksmith would say to his helpers, 'Right, let's try it,' and they would grasp the hot iron ring with long-handled tweezers, lift it out of the fire and lower it on to the wheel. With one deft movement and a bit of persuasion from the blacksmith, amid lots of smoke and the smell of burning wood, they were married together. Then buckets of water were gently splashed all round the wheel and tyre, to shrink the iron, one of the men told me. 'That won't come off in a hurry,' remarked the blacksmith. 'Come on, let's go and have one.' In every village I have lived in, I have never known the inn and the blacksmith's shop to be too far apart – not too much trouble for them to 'go and have one'.

In later years I have often marvelled at the skill of those village craftsmen, making two cumbersome wooden and iron articles in different parts of the village, then coming together, and without any fuss or bother, everything fitting. What family know-how had been handed down to them by their fathers and grandfathers, so different from nowadays when you call in the specialist repair man to repair your washing machine etc. Nothing fits. 'Sorry Sir, you need a new one, can't get any spares to fit this model,' and for this bit of information you are charged the earth.

To get back to Uncle Harry and his smart trap and high-stepping horse; both Uncle and Aunt insisted that Mother and Dad went for a drive in the countryside each day, they would say, 'Go into town, go and see so-and so; there is such a lovely ride through the forest, you can come back the main-road way and call on your dad's brother, he is getting on a bit and will be glad to see you.' And so, nearly every day, they went for their drive. They asked me many times to go with them, but I was happy on the smallholding, helping Uncle and Aunt. Unfortunately, they had no children of their own, so you can imagine how spoilt I was.

Looking back, I can see that it was better for my parents to be on their own. After being apart for five years, with the exception of brief leaves, they must have had so much to talk about. When they returned in the evening, after a meal and a rest, Dad would join Uncle in the bar. What better way to forget the hardship of war than sitting in a country pub bar with a glass of beer, talking to friends and feeling tired and relaxed after a good day's outing? Mother and Aunt would sit chatting for a time, then go outside to shut up the hens and look at the pigs.

Pigs were Aunt's speciality, her pride and joy. Although she told me many times how much she loved me, and that she was going to leave everything to me, I was of the firm opinion that if she had to choose between me and the old mother pig, the old mother pig would win the day. This old pig had been so spoilt by Aunt, I'm sure it thought it was one of the family. When we went for a walk in the village, she would amble along with us, and if we stopped to talk, she would stop too, and root about, all the time making contented little grunting noises. I have an old photograph of Aunt sitting on the village green with the old pig lying by her side. Aunt Ada is smiling into the camera, and I'm sure I can detect a smile on the face of the pig. What happened to her in the end, I don't know, but I bet they never ate her!

Uncle and Aunt eventually left the pub and had a nice little bungalow built on the smallholding – just right for them to take their ease in. She would say to me, 'This will be yours one day.' I didn't take too much notice of this. I would laugh and say, 'What about your old pig? You mustn't let her down!' Uncle would pull my leg if I became unwilling to do as I was told. 'Now then, young fellow, if you upset your aunt it will put a monkey on the chimney as far as you're concerned – watch it!' Thank goodness, they both lived to a ripe old age, and I went to stay with them on holiday for years.

At last our long holiday came to an end, and we returned to our own village. Father resumed his police duties, and we were all happy together. I began to realise how much I had missed the guiding hand of a man; you can be surrounded by aunts and thoroughly spoilt – all very nice, but things are so different between a boy and his father. I can remember the sense of belonging to him when we went fishing in the mill-stream for the first time, not the sophisticated fishing I had experienced with Mr Woodford, with all his superb fishing tackle, but with two rods cut out of the hedge, a length of strong thread, a bent pin and a worm. This was a game and it didn't matter if you made mistakes, you could have a good laugh. No sooner had we put our bait in the water than we caught a gudgeon, and we pulled gudgeons out of the stream one after the other. They were not hooked on to the pins, but were just hanging on to the worms, and we threw them all back. We had a drink at the miller's house and then made our way home – such comradeship. It was the same when we went for bike rides – my bike, by the way, was a second-hand one that Dad had arranged for me to pick up at the cycle repairer's. When I collected it, it had been freshly painted with black enamel which hadn't dried. My clothes were smothered with paint and we had to give the bike a coat of Judge's enamel at 6d a tin to cover it up.

We also had lots of trips to Northampton together, and I

felt so proud of this tall man, my father, in his uniform with medal ribbons on his chest, looking so immaculate. We went mainly to a cinema in Gold Street, which has disappeared long since. (I think it was turned into a penny bazaar, in other words, nothing was over a penny – an absolute shopping delight for children. I can remember it always being packed, both with goods and customers.) When we reached the cinema, a commissionaire stood outside, looking very smart in a gold braided uniform, a very imposing figure. As we entered the door which he was holding open for us, he and my father recognised one another.

'Hello Jim,' said Dad, 'I haven't seen you for years.'

'No,' said Jim, 'I retired several years ago and took this job for beer money. I'll see you again when you come out.' Dad explained to me that Jim was an old colleague and was just about to retire when he, Dad, joined the Force. Dad often met him in Angel Lane, where he had a desk job, and thought him a nice old boy.

When we came out of the cinema, Jim was waiting for us, and said to Dad, 'If ever your wife's in town shopping, and doesn't know what to do with the boy, tell her to bring him to me and I'll find a free seat for him,' and so he did. Nearly every time Mother took me to town, she would hand me over to Jim and he would march me into the cinema and sit me down, with strict instructions not to move. There I would sit, shouting at the top of my voice (they were silent pictures then), cheering the hero, and booing the villain, until this majestic figure came to claim me, telling me that my mother was waiting for me, and out I would go into the sunlight to Mum, bursting at the seams with excitement. This arrangement worked very well; free pictures for me, and Mother not having to put up with a reluctant shopper. I often say that it isn't what you know, it's who you know, and I was glad Dad knew Jim.

Dad also took me to the cinema regularly. It had been discovered that I had too many teeth, and this meant numerous trips to the dentist to have the extra teeth extracted one at a time, and a plate fitted to push the others into shape. My bribe for being brave at the dentist's was a visit to the cinema, so I watched Mutt and Jeff and all those old cartoons with great glee, with my mouth closed and bloody but my feet free to stamp in unison with the plot.

My father told me how he came to join the army as a young man. He began like this: 'I was the youngest of five children and we lived in a small village close to Kettering. My father worked on the land for a very low wage. Fortunately, my mother was a good needlewoman, and helped to raise the family income by sewing, but, like everyone else, we were very hard up. My three sisters went, as was expected of them in those days, into service and my brother Jim, who was not keen on farm work (I think he could see what Dad had to put up with), went into a boot and shoe factory in Kettering, and was soon earning nearly as much as his father. When it was time for me to leave school, I was persuaded to join him in the factory – Jim was able to get me a job, which was no mean task, because jobs were hard to find – and so, into the factory I went.

'I didn't like the factory work, but I stuck it for some years. I became friendly with a boy called Ginger, who also disliked being in a factory, and we made plans to leave the boot trade, but to no avail; there seemed to be no escape. We frequently failed to clock on; shoe workers are noted for that, they are an independent lot, and they wouldn't work if they had money in their pockets. "Cobbler's Monday" is proof of this. One day, when we were dodging work, Ginger asked me what I thought about joining the army. "I'm only just turned seventeen," was my reply, "you have to be eighteen before they will take you." "Never mind," said Ginger, "we are both big chaps, we'll say we're eighteen years old."

'So off we went to the recruiting office and asked to join the army. The recruiting sergeant told us we were just the type of chap he wanted, and before you could say "Jack Robinson", we were in the Artillery.

'After saying goodbye to the folks at home, we went to the Artillery depot and were put through our paces and were eventually, because of our size, sent to join the Royal Garrison Artillery. You had to be big and strong to handle sixty-pound shells. When we were at one depot we had to pick a mess mate – this was because two dinners were served on one plate. Needless to say, Ginger wasn't my choice for a mess mate – you tried to find a little chap, hoping he wouldn't eat too much! I remember once when we were on weapon training, we were being taught how to take various sights. One chap was not taking much notice and the instructor said to him, "Hi you! What's a fine sight?" to which the day-dreaming soldier replied, "Two dinners on one plate, Sir!" This remained a joke with us for years.

'Eventually, Ginger and I had done our three years active

service, both of us earning stripes, and out of the army we came on the reserves. After a time I missed the army life and looked around for something else to do. Whilst in the army I had taken advantage of their educational system and had gained a first class Certificate of Education. I thought about joining the police and asked Ginger what his feelings were about this, but he was not at all interested, so off I went and was accepted by the Police Force. After doing my basic training I was sent to Rushden, where I served under your grandfather, and met his daughter, your mother. After a time we were married, and I was given my first country assignment to the village where you were born.

'You will remember that, because I was still on the army reserve when war started, I had to report to my old unit at once, and there I again met Ginger, and after being put through our paces, we were allocated to different batteries. Mine was the 121st Heavy Battery with sixty-pounder guns and eight horses to pull them. We were then shipped off to France and Belgium. Things were very frustrating in Belgium – you could see our infantry in front of you, so hard pressed, and our guns were so short of shells it was impossible to give the support that was so badly needed, and at one time we were rationed to five shells a day. We would stack them in a pyramid and, for something to do, would metal polish the cases. It was bad for morale to stand about and take no part in the battle. At last more shells arrived and we were able to take a more active part in the fighting, trying to knock out the enemy's long-range guns which were shelling our troops so unmercifully.'

I was told so little about the actual horror of war, just isolated instances and funny anecdotes, and it was not until later in life that I heard the more gruesome details. One thing I do know, Dad was in an enormous number of engagements, and he had a chart given to him, as the Battery Sergeant Major of the 121st Battery. Mother had it framed and I am sure I have counted nearly sixty engagements on it. I will check when next I go to my son's house, as it now hangs on his wall for his three sons to see and marvel at. I asked about Ginger, had he come through the war safe and sound? In answer to this, Dad told me a funny little tale.

Half-way through the war, both he and Ginger – they both held the same rank – were offered commissions. They talked it over and Dad, knowing that a lieutenant's chance of being killed or wounded was above average, said, 'No, a live sergeant major is better than a dead lieutenant,' and so refused the promotion. Ginger, on the other hand, accepted, and they lost contact with one another.

Dad continued with a smile: 'During the latter part of the war Jerry made a big push; it could have been a last desperate effort and he was pushing us back at an alarming pace; our casualties were heavy and we began to get disorganised. Our infantry was coming back through our lines in a sorry state, and my captain said to me, "Sergeant Major, we must stop Jerry or he will cut our chaps off, follow me," and he went forward to the top of a ridge where he could see the advancing Germans. He shouted the range for me to relay back to the guns and gave the order to fire. He observed where the shells fell, and called to me, "Down fifty, fire!" After a moment I had the order to down another fifty. "That's good," said the captain, "we've got them on the run, drop another fifty, good shooting, they're running, drop another fifty!" These orders I relayed to my willing gunners, and they were firing as fast as they could. I knew we had not got the enemy on the run, by having to lower the range, indeed it was obvious that they were running towards us.

'We came under very heavy machine gun and rifle fire and had to pull back. At last my captain told me to hook the guns up and I gave my chaps the order to retreat, taking my horse, and the captain taking his. The captain, brave man that he was, didn't want to leave, and we left it nearly too late as we were almost surrounded. We managed to get away and made off at a gallop, hoping to catch up with our battery, but somehow the captain and I became separated and I was on my own, it was sheer hell! My horse was hit badly and I had to put him out of his misery with my revolver, then off I started to run. Unfortunately, I was wearing some officer-type boots of which I was very proud and which my batman took particular pride in, keeping them highly polished, but alas, they were not suitable for walking and running in, and my feet hurt so much they began to swell, making it almost impossible for me to hobble along. Every time I took a rest a shell would come over and up I would jump and run on. I was so tired and hot, hardly able to put one foot in front of the other, and I grew desperate. I flung myself down, fed up to the back teeth, determined not to budge another yard. If I'm captured, I thought I can't help it.

'It was then that I heard a horse cantering down the road and I thought it was an advance scout for the Germans, but as the horseman drew nearer I saw he was British, in fact, a British major. I stepped out into the road and the major said, "Well, well, well! You?" I took a good look at his mud-splashed face and "My God!" I said, "Ginger!" "Get up behind me," said Ginger, "I'll soon have us both out of this," and off we went at a smart pace to comparative safety. We were able to talk – Ginger told me he had been cut off from his unit; had had to make a detour, and had almost given up hope when he saw me. "By the way," he said, tapping his major's crown, "how's this for a dead lieutenant? Not bad, eh?" Using his major's rank he soon found a horse for me and I was able to join what was left of my unit.'

When I asked Dad if he ever saw Ginger again, he said they kept in touch for some years, but because Ginger was discharged from the army with the rank of major, he was able to get a good job and he had got on in the world, moving about all over the place, so that they had lost contact with each other. I should have liked to meet this Ginger to thank him for saving my dad. What a remarkable true tale of those two meeting like that; it could almost be made into a play.

The only injury my father suffered during the war was being gassed slightly; he told me it happened like this: 'One day we were giving support to some French-Portuguese infantry who were having a particularly bad time from German shelling. We were trying to pinpoint the German guns and knock them out, but visibility grew worse and we could see a mist coming up, mixing with the smoke of battle; this mist thickened up into a thick fog and came rolling towards us. Very soon the French-Portuguese came running through our lines in a dreadful state, their hands covering their eyes as they coughed and spluttered, shouting to us, "Asphyxiant, Monsieur! Asphyxiant, Monsieur!" as they ran by us. We were rather put out at them running away, and tried to stop them, but all to no avail. In a short time, this fog enveloped us, and in no time at all, we too were coughing, with our eyes streaming, and we also beat a hasty retreat. This must be the gas that we had heard rumours about, but had never encountered before. It was most demoralising – you can't fight a cloud of gas, and we had no protection at all from this vile method of waging war. After we escaped from this poisonous cloud we were in a sorry state. I was a casualty and, unable to see, was marched back to the dressing station, bandaged and labelled, and sent back to England. From there I went by train to Scotland and to a Scottish castle for treatment. Thank goodness, my dose of gas was not too severe, and I recovered remarkably well.

'I was sent back to France to rejoin my unit, making the crossing on a troopship packed with soldiers from the Highlands of Scotland, most of them Gaelic speaking. We docked at a port in Brittany and the local dockworkers were rushing about to get us docked quickly, shouting instructions to one another in the local dialect which, to the amazement of the Gaelic-speaking Scots who were looking over the side of the ship, they could understand, and very quickly conversation was flowing between them. There must be a common Celtic ancestry somewhere along the line – most interesting.

'When I rejoined my unit there had been a lot of changes; casualties had been high and there were many new replacements. A large number of these replacements were from the Cardiff City Police Force – such splendid fellows. I was the smallest in the sergeants' mess, and you know I'm six foot tall. How they sang! They made it a rule in the mess when we were off duty that you had to sing a song or pay for the drinks all round. Needless to say, I soon learnt to sing, much to the amusement of my Welsh comrades, who howled like dogs when I was in full voice. It took a bit of doing, to sing in front of that lot!

'It was because of the enthusiasm of my Welsh friends that I nearly had a ticket back to dear old Blighty. I was forward of our guns with my field-glasses, trying to get the range, and standing under what was left of a big old tree, when my battery let off a round prematurely, hitting the old tree I was standing under, smashing it to pieces and bowling me over in the process. Where I had been standing was a huge part of the trunk and I had missed death by inches – this time from my own mates.

'When I was back home recovering from the effects of the gas, I discovered that your Uncle Albert was in the field artillery, and had been for some time. I found out where he was, which was quite close to me, and when I returned to my unit, I got in touch with his battery commander and he was given permission to visit me. I'm glad I did, for he was rather down in the dumps. His unit had just been through a rough patch, and although he had tried to smarten himself up to come and see me, he looked pretty rough. My good friend, the quartermaster sergeant, told me to leave him to him and he'd square him up, and so he did, with new clothes from top to bottom – what a difference! I got permission for him to join me in the sergeants' mess, and in no time at all we had him singing – he sang rather well, as a matter of fact. When it was time for him to leave, we wished one another well, saying, "See you back in Blighty after this lot's over," each of us, no doubt, wondering what the chances were of this happening.' Fortunately, Uncle Albert did come through the war safe and sound, and he and Dad had many a tale to tell each other. Uncle often told me how much he had enjoyed being a gunner in the sergeants' mess.

My father told me of an unusual position he found himself in during an advance the British were making. (It may not have been so unusual when you think about it.) He said there had been a terrific battle and bombardment for days in bitter weather, when gradually the enemy began to fall back. He was told to go forward and find some new positions for his guns – the idea was to keep Jerry on the move. In this forward position, which was littered with dead, he slipped in the mud and fell into a shell crater. There were several bodies in this crater, one of them being a young lieutenant, little more than a boy. He turned him over in order to get a better look at him, and lo and behold, he was not dead but just lying still, quietly crying. Dad asked him if he was hit anywhere and the answer was, 'No, I couldn't stand any more and I panicked – I was scared stiff and I ran.'

'Don't let that worry you too much,' said Dad. 'You are not the only one to do this. Buck yourself up, you can come back with me. We'll find your lot and nobody need know.'

'That's not the worst of it,' said the boy, 'I've also messed my pants.'

'This has happened to many a brave man,' replied that hardened campaigner, my father, 'take them off and throw them away – no one will know.' Dad went on to say that when he went back to base he took the boy with him and handed him over to his batman with instructions to clean the young fellow up and to give him a good drink of rum out of his water-bottle. Dad always said that when you were under heavy bombardment every sip of rum put another foot of concrete over your head, or so it felt. Dad told his officers he had found the young lieutenant knocked out and had brought him back. Before the young officer went off in search of his unit, by now feeling a better man, he took Dad's name and home address and gave Dad his own. He squeezed Dad's hand, looked him straight in the eyes and said, 'Thanks, I will write to you after the war,' which he did.

It would appear that he made a good soldier after that one lapse. Dad gathered from his letter that he had been promoted to captain before the end of the war. Apparently his family owned a shipping line, quite a well-known one. His letter ended by saying that if he could ever do anything for Dad or his family, 'do not hesitate to ask.'

I was asked in later years whether I resented my father coming home as I had had so much freedom and was maybe spoilt by my mother, aunts and grandparents. The answer to this is obvious – how could you resent such a man? I am only too pleased that at long last I have put down on paper some of the things I find so hard to say, before it is too late. Now my children and their children will have a better understanding of a grandfather and great grandfather who will not be just a faded photograph in the family album, or hanging on the house wall, but a live, brave soldier of the First World War.

Chapter 7

More Moves, More Villages, and a School With a Difference

Although we had become completely readjusted to post-war life, things, of course, would never be, and we could not expect them to be, the same. There were many gaps in families, caused by this dreadful war, with so much evidence of the cost to a nation's young men – villagers with limbs missing, some suffering from shell-shock. What a dreadful thing it was; people who were normal could not understand, and in some cases, did not try to understand, these poor unfortunate men. We had not heard much about nerves in those days, and to think that anyone could have them damaged to the extent of upsetting the co-ordination of their limbs and facial muscles, without being bodily injured, was hard to believe.

In a village community, so often closely related and inter-married, the odd case of someone being mentally retarded and unusual was taken for granted, and a place was found for them in village life, with no unfair advantages taken of them. I have known quite a few such people in different places and they nearly always appeared to be quite happy.

It was not until we were better informed, and read articles written by learned doctors, that it was realised that shell-shock was a condition brought about by the dreadful conditions of modern warfare, and must now be recognised as an injury sustained in war as much as having a leg blown off.

As I was saying, no sooner had we settled down to post-war life than Father was moved, this time to a village some miles to the north of Northampton – a rather more up-to-date, go-ahead place, with a modern, newly built school of which the village people were very proud. The school may have been up-to-date, but the police house was just the opposite – a poor little terraced house which had been left in a very sorry state. Really, there was no other way to describe the place than to say that it was dirty; the neighbours told us that the late tenant's wife was a very nice person but she read books all day. Making a move that we didn't want to make and arriving to find the house in such a state was not a good start to our life in a new village.

What a shock I had when I started school. I was asked what class I had been in when I left my old school and when I told them, was put in the same class in this school. I have never felt so ashamed in my life – I was so unaware of what the lessons were about that I was put into a lower class and after a day or two went even lower. Eventually, the teacher's young daughter was placed next to me to explain what was going on. Sitting next to a girl was bad enough, but to be sent down several classes was unbearable. I was so upset that my father went to see the headmaster, who told him I had either been taught incorrectly or had been neglected. He said it was so obvious that I was an intelligent boy, but that I could hardly grasp any of the subjects excepting art, at which I was good, and sport. He felt that if I worked hard I would soon catch up with my age group. I was so humiliated that for the first time in my life I worked hard at school, and was very soon promoted until I was in my rightful class – all done in a couple of months. Such a change came over me, I became interested in so many things and took advantage of what the school had to offer.

I became friendly with a quiet, studious boy and we did our homework together in his larger house, where we used a room set aside for our studies. He played the piano and violin very well indeed, and to the amazement of my parent, I asked if I could have piano lessons. This pleased them very much as they had often suggested piano lessons to me but always got a polite refusal, and here I was asking for lessons! Wonders would never cease. My friend and I practised the piano for hours, and, when we were not practising music, we were studying.

I can tell you so little about this village. I had no adventures there but took to school life as never before, and according to Mother, I also began to play the piano rather well, considering the length of time I had been receiving lessons. Looking back, I am sure I was not so happy there, and certainly not so carefree, as before my enlightenment. I now had to reason why, and not take things for granted. Although my stay in this village was comparatively short, as police posting goes, I must say it did me good.

My father was promoted to sergeant, and so we moved to another, quite large, Northamptonshire village. This time I was fully confident that whatever the educational standards expected of me by the new school I would soon attend, at least I would not be demoted, and this proved to be the case. There was just one hiccup. On the first day, as usual, the boys tested the ability of the policeman's son to protect himself. I was fully prepared for this, and when challenged, went into the attack at once, adopting an aggressive attitude; this paid off handsomely, because all the time I remained in this village, I just had the usual boyish punch-ups – no taking it out of the policeman's boy!

It is surprising, in this county of squires and spires, how the villages and the characters of the villagers are so different and yet still remain so unmistakably Northamptonshire. I have often said that the Northamptonshire Uplands compare favourably with the Cotswolds. All over the county you unexpectedly come upon pretty villages, and the countryside can never be described as uninteresting. This new village I had moved to was a mixture of old and new houses but it did not let the county down when it came to church spires. What a magnificent church, with a towering spire – I could sit in my class at school and gaze at this link with the past. I was soon informed by other children that it was the second oldest church in England and I can quite believe it.

After I had been living there for some little time, I was enrolled in the choir. I would sit in the choir stalls and look around the ancient church, with its gallery, and marvel that it had stood so long. One Sunday, my daydreams were shattered during the sermon by a most unusual noise, coming from the part of the church behind the organ where the boys sat pumping the bellows which supplied the air to the instrument. Twin brothers had this job, and on this Saturday they were fighting ferociously. They were big, strong boys, and because they were twins, were also well matched. The choir master intervened, but this seemed to make things worse, and as the sound of fighting became louder, the rector lost the trend of his sermon and you could see the congregation's attention wavering. The poor rector had to come down from the pulpit to give the choir master a hand in his efforts to part the pugalistic organ blowers – all very entertaining for we choir boys.

This was a village in the heart of the Pytchley country and very much steeped in hunting – the home of the Pytchley hounds. I remember being awakened on my first night there by a most unearthly clamour, unlike any noise I had ever heard before; it made cold shivers run down my spine. I went into my parents' room and they, too, were awake. 'What is it?' I asked, and my father replied, 'It sounds as if it's coming from the kennels,' and, indeed, it was. Many of the hounds were fighting, and very soon we heard mens' voices, the cracking of whips, and a few yelps, after which peace was restored.

We wondered how often this happened during the night, as our house was quite close to the kennels, and we were to discover that these pack fights were quite frequent. But we soon became used to them, and if we were woken up we managed to get back to sleep again quite easily. Talk about the Hound of the Baskervilles! When the breeding bitches were in pup, they had a certain amount of freedom, and at times were allowed to roam about the village. You seldom saw them in pairs – nearly always one bitch on her own, slinking about like a thief in the night, and what expert thieves they were. Heaven help a housewife who had left food on the table and her door open – it was gone in a flash. It was not eaten on the spot, the thieves always made a quick exit, with whatever they had stolen held in their mouths, and no amount of shouting or throwing of stones would make them drop their loot. I saw one with a dainty cream jug, full of cream, carrying it very carefully back to the kennels, so unlike any other kind of dog, which would have broken the jug and licked up the cream on the spot. The hounds were so large that they were able to reach things off the pantry shelves (no deep freezers in those days). I remember one woman in tears, coming to report the theft of her Sunday dinner, which she had left on the table in the baking tin, ready to put in the oven. It was a blessing that the hunt master always settled any claims without hesitation; nevertheless, the hounds were a constant threat to the unwary housewife.

It was a pleasing sight to see the whips, on foot, exercising a whole pack of these robust hounds. One man walked at a fast pace in front and the other brought up the rear, with constant naming of any miscreants, and if they did not obey at once, a flick of the long-lashed whip, which both men carried, would ensure that complete control was maintained. I've seen people taking one little dog for a walk have less control, even if it's on a lead. Some of the older hounds had young hounds chained to them, and it was easy to see that the old hound was the boss. Naturally, whenever a meet was held close to us, we always went.

I may have become accustomed to the fighting of the hounds at night, but one disadvantage of living near hunt kennels was the smell of food being prepared for the hounds. Most weeks, and sometimes several times a week, the knacker's man would take a dead animal into the kennels, usually a dead horse, and this would be boiled and fed to the hounds. If the wind was in the wrong quarter, a most unpleasant smell of cooking would be wafted around for the best part of the day. It was impossible to escape from this smell, even indoors. This, of course, must have changed over the years, and a more up-to-date method used for the preparation of food for the hounds.

In one of the cottages near to us, lived an old man who, I think, did earth stopping before a meet, but his speciality was badgers. There were nearly always badger skins hanging on his clothes-line in the process of being cured. He had two rough-haired Sealyham terriers, specially trained for the cruel sport of badger-baiting, but actually, as far as he was concerned, I don't think it was a sport; I have an idea he was paid to clear a farmer's land of this misunderstood animal. I know farmers had an idea that badgers killed lambs and were guilty of spreading tuberculosis. One day I was asked whether I would like to accompany him on his badger hunt, but after taking a good look at his oldest dog, called Jack, and noting that he had one ear missing – the other was just a mangled ball – no sight in one eye, his lips torn away so that his teeth were always exposed, and just a morsel of a nose left, I declined with a shudder. At least, I thought, old Brock gives a good account of himself.

Most unusual for a village, we had what was known in those days as a workhouse. This was an imposing, stone-faced building with pillars to the front, giving the impression of a gentleman's house, so unlike the usual run of dreary, red-bricked, Dickensian buildings seen in many towns. I think it is used today as a local council building, and if this is so, I wonder, when the committee is sitting, trying to balance the budget, if anyone spares a thought for, or is reminded of, the children of sixty-five years ago, to whom this building was home.

I can recall the workhouse children attending our school. It was the understood thing, no doubt drummed into us by our teachers, that we should be kind to them, as unlike the rest of us, they had no mothers or fathers. (Could this be the result of the war?) I felt so sorry for them; they were dressed so differently from we village children. The boys wore short smocks and short trousers made from stiff grey calico with thin black stripes, and their hair was cut so short, it looked as if clippers had been used. The girls wore frocks of the same material, with aprons, I think, and their hair was also cut very short, although not shorn off like the boys. I felt especially sorry for them, because it was the fashion for the girls to wear their hair long in those days. I remarked on this to my mother, who said it was probably better to be cut short – so much easier to keep clean, and didn't I remember the nits she sometimes combed out of my hair? If you had lots of girls with long tresses, it would be difficult to keep their heads clean. I saw the logic in this, particularly on days when the sun streamed through the school windows and shone on the heads of the girls sitting in front of me, clean girls from good homes, but you could see the little beasts running about. Their hair was full of lice, and so was mine – thank goodness those days are over – or are they? I sometimes wonder when you see the new styles adopted by the youth of today, which look to me like ideal breeding grounds. Hygiene was so strict with the workhouse children. I remember the strong smell of carbolic when they marched into class. Death to all germs!

I recall being friendly with the workhouse master's daughter, and being asked to visit the family for tea. This was an eye-opener for me as I had expected a prison-like atmosphere, but I have never seen anything less like a prison; it gave me the impression of being in one large, well-organised family unit, playing all kinds of games in which we all joined. I think, as far as humanly possible, the workhouse children were happy – a feather in the cap of the staff, I would say.

Directly opposite our house across the main road, was a rather large house enclosed on the roadside by a high wall. Inside was a very secluded garden with an orchard and paddock. The gentleman who lived there seemed to me to live a very quiet, studious life, hardly ever coming out into the village, so you can imagine my surprise when one day he came across to our cottage and asked my parents if I might be allowed to play with his son, who was home from boarding school and was lonely and needed young company. My parents agreed, saying it would keep me out of trouble during the long summer holidays. So off I went with this gentleman and was introduced to his son who was about my age, a very pleasant boy who was obviously glad to see me. He took me into his room and showed me his toys, games, books etc. I was quite fascinated by his collection of birds' eggs, not so much by the numbers he had, but by the way they were stored and presented. Each egg had its own green baize compartment in a wooden tray with handles, was neatly labelled, and tray after tray fitted into a bureau. Nearly every boy in those days collected birds' eggs, and mine were kept in shoe boxes, either resting on cotton wool or fine sawdust. No attempt was made to label them, and so often, when being handled, they would break; this invariably happened to the rarest of them.

After a long talk about birds and their eggs, I was asked if I would like to see his rifle range. This sounded most interesting; what boy wouldn't jump at the chance of being shown anything remotely connected with guns? To my amazement, a perfect small arms rifle range was laid out in the orchard, with an ideal shed to fire from. The front of the shed lifted up and a strong wooden bar was fitted across it at the correct height to rest your arm on to take aim. There were tables and chairs so that onlookers could take their ease whilst watching the shooting – absolutely ideal. Fifty yards or more away was a tall earth bank with boards to pin your target on – so safe. I was told that we had to be supervised by the boy's father when firing rifles, but we could use air guns on our own. I could not wait to try my hand at this, and in no time at all two BSA rifles were produced, with tins of lead pellets. After the targets were fastened half-way up the range, I was instructed how to load, take aim and fire, cautioned never, ever, to point the gun at anyone, even if it was not loaded; never to go out of the firing shed unless we all went; to keep my finger off the trigger, etc., etc. So I had a good grounding in small arms safety at an early age, and this I never forgot. I had one bad lapse during the Second World War, over which I lost a few nights sleep. One day, in my excitement, I stepped in front of a tommy gun that hadn't finished firing – never again! Back to my boyhood initiation into guns. It was found that I was a natural shot – I hit the bull's-eye with ease after the first few shots. My new friend, Timothy, called his father and showed him my targets. 'We'll see how he gets on with a real rifle,' he said, and unlocked a strong room and brought out two .22 rifles and ammunition. Once again I was put through the safety drill and told in no uncertain way that these rifles were lethal weapons and could kill. Timothy's father said, 'Never point one of these at anyone unless you want to kill him,' and I have always remembered this. After I became accustomed to the noise and slight kick-back, I made an excellent shot.

After weeks of practice, Timothy and I, with the aid of telescopic sights, would wait for flies to settle on different targets, and kill them. This gift of hitting the target never left me, no matter what type of weapon I used. I remember before the Second World War, I was at a shooting gallery, and I had five shots at a target, without apparently taking much aim. When my target was wound down to me, I was told I had one in the bull and the other four I had missed completely, but after looking at the target, I could see all five had gone thereabouts through the one hole, and the booth proprietor had to agree that this was so. He went on to say that the test of good shooting was to bend the target into an L shape and split the edge, and he wagered ten shillings (50p) I couldn't do it. I dared not back down, and although I could ill afford to lose ten shillings, I accepted. I took aim and fired my five shots at the edge of the target, hoping I had split it with one shot. When it was wound down to me, to my amazement, and the booth owner's dismay, I had split the target three times.

Although I had great fun with Timothy during the school holidays, I was not sorry when Dad said that we were going to be moved once again. I have always found that some villages you like, others you just put up with, and the latter was the case with Timothy's village. I only had one other friend there, the butcher's son, Jeff, and, as was the custom in those days, he had to help his father a great deal. One of his chores was to clean pigs' guts in salt water, turning them inside out and running clean warm water through them until they were spotless. So that we could get off to play, I would help with this boring task, and I often think about it when we have sausages today. I bet Jeff was glad when artificial sausage skins were invented! It was a messy job and didn't make my feelings for the village any warmer. I wondered what the next village would have in store.

Chapter 8

How Good to be Involved in the Life of a Military Establishment and Still Be Able to Go Home to Sleep

One day we were having our evening meal after Dad had been to Police Headquarters on pay-day. This monthly visit was combined with drill and inspection and the usual pep talks. He was so meticulous in his dress, with trousers pressed, boots and buttons polished like glass and always making sure he had his warrant card, notebook and pencil, whistle, handcuffs and truncheon, etc. We always felt proud of him and confident that his superiors would have little cause for complaint or to criticise him on his appearance. We all looked forward to these monthly pay-days, Mother, for obvious housekeeping reasons – a month between pay-days took a lot of budgeting for – and I looked forward to my sweets and small presents, brought back with such unfailing regularity. Dad also enjoyed going; he met his mates, talked shop and repaired to the hostelry, which was invariably very close to the main police station. As a rule, a rather select room was kept for these gatherings.

I remember, when I was old enough to drive my Father's huge 8 h.p. motor cycle and two-seater side-car, and he had received a knee injury in the course of his duties, I was asked to be his chauffeur on pay-days. I quite enjoyed this as it meant that I could spend time looking around, and perhaps sneaking off for a ride around the countryside. My instructions were to pick Dad up at a certain time, and to go in for a lemonade and a packet of biscuits. I did not need to be asked twice or told where to go. It was so pleasant to see this room full of comrades, off duty, happy and relaxed, with a pint before them – such imposing men. No wonder a clip round the ear with their gloves, or a stern warning given, was, in most cases, sufficient to keep law and order without recoursing to a summons and getting people fined five shillings or more for their misdemeanours. These fines, and a day off work, they could ill afford – the public knew this and accepted the on-the-spot reprimand. I think we were all the better for it. Nowadays, when I see that colourful series of etchings of policemen in various places, mostly country hotels, I look at the one entitled '9 Pints of the Law', and I can't help giving a little chuckle, remembering those far-off pay-days and Petty Sessions.

To get back to our evening meal. Dad, on this occasion, seemed unusually quiet. Mother sensed that something was wrong; 'What is it?' she enquired.

'We have got to move again,' my father replied. Now Father always tried to prepare Mother and me for our forthcoming moves, and I think it helped. We always felt dismay at the thought of leaving the friends we had made, the house and garden we had worked on and felt so proud of. I immediately began to think of another school – what would the masters be like and would they like me? My tummy began to turn over. I know as a child I disliked changes, and still do to this day. I am sure Mother felt the same. From Dad's description of this new village, it seemed so unlike any of our previous homes.

Dad began by describing the house we would be living in. This was a small, self-contained police station housing three men. The centre block had three cells, an office and a charge room. Over the cells were quarters for a single constable which had a front entrance. This block was flanked on either side by two adjoining houses – our house was on the right of the block and a married constable lived in the other one. The constable's wife cooked for and looked after the single constable. The house would be rather noisy as, although it stood well back from the road, the main London to Birmingham road passed the gates. Solid-tyred lorries bumped and clanked by unceasingly, day and night. Many of these lorries were ex-army, not built for quiet running, and there were also quite a few steam lorries among them. These, unfortunately, always seemed to run out of steam outside our house which was built on a steep hill. After the drivers had stoked the fires up and raised steam, with lots of shouting going on, the lorries would slowly puff off, sparks flying everywhere. (All this information Dad had received from the sergeant he was relieving.)

I saw Mother pull a face. 'It seems as if we are not going to get much sleep at night until we become accustomed to the change,' she said. Father went on to say that that was not all, 'We shall be surrounded by horses and soldiers – hundreds go trotting by each day, and over our back-garden wall you will see other soldiers being taught tent-pegging and riding full tilt at dummy men, piercing them with either swords or lances, and at the same time uttering blood-curdling cries, to the encouragement, or sometimes otherwise, of leather-lunged instructors.' My ears cocked up when I heard all this, and I promised myself that I would spend some time looking over our garden wall. Dad went on, 'Just below us, in a large walnut plantation, are thirty Metropolitan police bungalows. They have nothing to do with the county police, they look after a large ordnance stores depot, employing lots of civilians, mostly old soldiers, to look after millions of rifles, machine guns, etc. These are tested in batches at different times of the day and are quite noisy, as a matter of fact.'

'It sounds super to me,' I said, very excited at the prospect of watching all this military carry-on, so unlike the quiet country villages we had lived in before. I was reminded of Gramp's house, with soldiers training close by, several years ago. 'Don't look so pleased, young fellow,' said Dad, 'you will have a mile and a half to run to school – no lying in bed until the last minute – and about a mile to fetch the milk from a farm along the road, making two miles there and back, and with coming home from school at lunchtime (no school dinners then), you will do six miles to and from school plus two miles for the milk, making eight miles a day! That should keep you fit.'

The moving day arrived. This was an upsetting, muddled sort of day; the County, in its wisdom, only hired one lorry to do two or three moves in one day. If you were first on the list things were not too bad – you packed your belongings into an empty lorry to start with, but it was not so easy when you arrived at your destination and you had to clear the house of the departing family's furniture before you were able to unload yours. If it rained it was most unpleasant as your furniture and bedding could not be kept dry – so worrying for Mums. I do think the County let their men down in those days with such penny-pinching.

As I grew older I thought of the houses we had lived in, rented by the County to house its country policemen. They may have been picturesque, but my word, so many were lacking in the bare essentials. We expected and quite enjoyed pumping our water, when we met our neighbours and had a chat around the communal pump, and we were convinced that well water was so pure. This may have been true in some cases, but at times, seeing what was dumped and spilt around the wells, I had my doubts.

Sanitation in some of the houses was very primitive. In at least two of the houses supplied to us, the menfolk had to wash in bowls standing on benches outside the back door, and all your neighbours did the same; there was no sink in either of these cottages, and the women either washed upstairs at the bedroom wash-stand, or in a bowl on the kitchen table. The toilets, too, were very primitive indeed, and consisted of three seats placed over an earth pit, which was emptied once a year on a moonlit night! My eye! Keep those bedroom windows closed!! As I've said, I do feel the County could have done better for its police.

How pleased we were to find that this new home was up-to-date with running water. The water had to be pumped into a tank in the roof by a most unusual pump – it was a huge iron wheel standing at least six feet high which had to be turned by hand. This was placed just outside the cells, no doubt designed for punishment for the prisoners. When the cells were empty it was the duty of the constable to keep the tank full and I helped many times with this chore – it really did need two pairs of hands to pump for any length of time.

After we had settled in and were reasonably straight, a boy

of my age came to our door and told us he was the regimental sergeant major's son from the army bungalow next door. He offered to show me round the barracks and take me down to the other part of the village, where I would be going to school. I jumped at this offer, so we called for the cook sergeant's son and set off for the barracks. How different this was from anything I had ever seen before – a complete military establishment, teeming with soldiers and horses and strong-looking two-horse wagons being driven here and there. I was later to find out that these were known as GS wagons (General Service). I was advised by the other boys not to walk across the barracks square, but to go round the perimeter. We were also to stand still if addressed by an officer or senior NCO. The sergeant major's son said I was not to be surprised if his father and others shouted at us to take our hands out of our pockets, but not to worry as their bark was worse than their bite. This was demonstrated to me when we visited the cookhouse; everyone was so busy, but when the cook sergeant saw us he sent out three huge wedges of pie, with instructions to eat it and not to be seen eating it. It tasted super.

Our next port of call was the gymnasium, and a very tall PT instructor broke off from putting a squad of men through their paces and came over to us. He was told I was the new policeman's son and I was asked if I would like to join the other boys for boxing lessons and gymnastics. My new friends answered for me, saying that I would, and that is how I became involved with the gym for five and a half years, and I enjoyed every moment of it.

We next visited the stables which seemed to me miles long, full of horses and with not a wisp of hay out of place.

The cobbled floor was clean enough to eat off – so unlike any stables I had ever seen before, and there were rows upon rows of them. There must have been several thousand horses, or so it seemed to me.

I was taken to see the RSM's special mount known as Daddy Long Legs. The walls of his box were simply covered with rosettes which he had won for jumping at events all over the country. I was told to be wary of him as he was very playful. One of his tricks was to grab your hat with his teeth, often taking a mouthful of hair at the same time – very painful – and dropping it in his water bucket. When I became better acquainted with his old civilian groom, I often noticed that he had a black eye, given to him, he assured us, by the old hoss! We rather thought he liked his half-pint too much and maybe expressed himself too forcibly when in the company of others. We boys knew when to keep out of his way. That 'old hoss' was a superb jumper and was entered for jumping competitions all the time.

The sergeants' mess organised outings for themselves and their families and Mother and Father and me were included. Father was, by then, an honorary member of the sergeants' mess. One of our outings was to Olympia to cheer Daddy Long Legs on. Unfortunately, or so we thought, he was not being ridden by the RSM but by a young officer, who let him play up, you could almost say show off, to the crowd, and he consequently came in third. We followed him to County shows and agricultural shows, and never, ever, did he let us down but that once.

We also went by special train to the Royal Tournament with horses and troops who were putting on trick riding, tent-pegging and pig-sticking displays. How proud we felt of our 'boys', who gave such a faultless display, watched by hundreds of people, and how we cheered. When the show was over we went behind the scenes and met up with our crowd. Most of the men disappeared, to return later with glowing, red faces; it could have been the excitement or the heat which gave them such a look of well-being – but somehow I think not.

Before the show started, my father took me to see the Royal Artillery display team and guns. He was full of praise for the immaculate turn-out, commenting, 'These chaps have worked hard and well, a credit to old Artillery men everywhere.' I am sure he wore his Artillery tie with additional pride.

As I write this, my mind goes back to a grand old man who lived fifty years ago in my present village. He lived in a row of very old thatched cottages, more or less touching the roadside. This old man's cottage had what I can only describe as a stable door – the top half could be opened while the bottom half remained closed; this was ideal for keeping children in and animals out. It also served Harry, for this was the grand old man's name, as a support, as he could put his arms over the top of the closed half of the door. 'It helps to rest me poor old legs, boy,' he would say to me, and he was also able to chat to everyone who passed by. At odd times I would see him out in the village, struggling along on two stout sticks, making his way down to the Rose and Crown. One morning I popped into the bar of the Rose and Crown and there sat Harry by the fire, in a huge armchair, with an empty pint pot at his elbow.

'Would you like another?' I asked.

'Yes, boy, I would,' said Harry.

When I took his pint over to him, he grasped it by the handle, struggled to his feet, held the pint high, stood to attention, and in a round voice said, 'The right of the line, the pride of the line, the British Royal Artillery. God bless the King!' With that, he put his pint to his lips and the contents disappeared at one go – I didn't even see his Adam's apple move. He fixed me with his watery, pale blue eyes and said, 'That's how an Artillery man drinks the Royal Toast.'

After I had got my breath back – his seemed all right – I said, 'You're an old gunner, then?'

'Yes, boy, many years ago and because I was such a good horseman I was put into the King's Troop, Royal Artillery. Eventually I was made a corporal and we put on all kinds of demonstrations and tournaments at all kinds of events, firing the Royal Salute, etc. We went all over the country. We had to train hard and I can remember galloping around the barracks square for hours, until we got it right. I had a pal who would slip into the corporals' mess, come out with a quart of ale and hold it out for me to take when next I came round. I grabbed it, drank it up while cantering round the square, giving him the empty pot when I went by him. Took a bit of doing, that.' There were other times when I treated him and he always drank up 'like an Artillery man'. Eventually, his poor old legs would not take him out of the house, and he spent his last days looking over his door. I felt tempted to take him a pint, then I thought of his wife, who must have seen so many hard earned coppers' worth slip down his throat, and I chickened out. When I passed by his house I would shout out,

'The right of the line,' and he would finish it, chuckling all the time. These old characters are so sadly missed in a village.

Back to the Royal Tournament of my boyhood. So much hard work went on at the depot before these demonstrations of horse-riding skills could be put on before the Royal Family and other celebrities, foreign military attachés and hundreds of discerning people. I watched the preparations for tent-pegging and dummy-thrusting with sword and lance, from my garden wall; the trick riding and acrobatic riding I watched from the gallery of a huge, indoor riding school, often being joined there by very senior officers. I listened with interest to their comments, and so was able, more or less, to predict which rides would be chosen for the great day – all so very interesting.

Many years afterwards, just before the Second World War, I had helping me on my garden allotment, an ex-serviceman named Algy, who tried hard to make ends meet on an army disability pension. Poor Algy had a piece of shrapnel pass through his chest, coming out under his shoulder blade and piercing a lung in the process. This wound never healed properly and would constantly give him trouble.

Algy badgered me to let him work in the garden and I agreed on the understanding that he would be his own boss, coming when he liked, sitting down when he felt like it, and going home when he'd had enough. This arrangement worked out very well for Algy, subsidising his pension which was just over £1 a week – not much for beer and baccy. Algy took complete charge of the garden (half an acre), and woe betide me if I helped myself to some new potatoes without his permission. We sometimes had relations call in the summer in time for supper, and my wife would ask me to go to the garden for some spring onions, a lettuce or two, and a couple of roots of new potatoes. With my tongue in my cheek and my eye cocked for Algy, I would do this. The next day I was inevitably buttonholed by my head gardener, with, 'Who's been on my garden?'

'I have, Algy,' I would reply, waiting to be chastised. 'Hmm!! You! I thought it was a herd of bloody bullocks by the mess that's been made!'

He would moan to his old cronies in the Rose and Crown about how I always took things that were not ready, and they would enter into the spirit of things and pull my leg – all done with straight faces.

I know Algy appreciated us both, especially the wife, for every Christmas Day he would bring her a bunch of Christmas roses. It didn't matter what the weather was like, she had her roses. He would sit with a hot toddy in his hand, watching our children opening their Christmas presents, puffing his old twist tobacco, and fortified by several more hot rums and sugar, until the clock said midday, then, wishing us a Happy Christmas, he would be off and all was forgiven.

Why I thought about all this when I was describing the riding school at my military village, was because one day when we were chatting, I mentioned the riding school to Algy. He bucked up and said, 'I know it – I passed my riding course there before being shipped overseas, and when I was there, who do you think I ran into? Old Peter!' Now, old Peter was another of my help-mates, a character whose like I had never met before or since, a man upset by his war service, a morose sort of chap, with odd bursts of humour.

He suffered periods of deep depression, asking me, when these moods were upon him, to either lend him a gun or whatever, so that he might kill himself, or failing this, would I do it for him. I became quite adept with my replies to these requests, in as much as he worked with me and for me for a number of years, passing away eventually through illness, and in bed. I have so many lovely stories concerning Peter, all of them true, and none doing anyone any harm.

One of the strange things about Peter was that he could stand on his head, completely motionless, for hours on end. Many times I have had a 'phone call from some pub or other, asking me to 'Come and fetch old Peter – he's standing on his head on the table (or chair, or whatever) and we can't get him down. All he will say is 'phone you.' Off I would go, and sure enough, standing on his head, as steady as a rock, would be Peter. I would say, 'Come on, old lad, I'm here,' and down would come Peter, apparently none the worse after about an hour upside down! He would sit down beside me, suggesting that we have a couple of pints before we set off for home. After the two pints were consumed, we would make the short journey back to our own village, never mentioning the incident to one another.

When Algy said that he had met Peter in the army, at this indoor riding school, I listened all agog. Algy went on, 'Peter, the artful beggar, made out he couldn't ride, so he missed several drafts overseas. You know, as well as I do, that very few farm workers are unable to ride, but Peter had kidded them that he couldn't and that it would be better if they discharged him from the army. The army had different ideas and was determined to make a soldier of him. He was put with our new batch for basic riding lessons – this, I understand, was the third time for Peter, and we rode into the riding school together. We had a loud-voiced, rough-riding corporal as an instructor on that day, shouting and swearing at us all, particularly at old Peter, who was sitting his horse like a sack of potatoes tied up loose. My word, I thought, Peter you're going to get it in a minute. The corporal was called away, and he instructed us to carry on by ourselves until he came back. No sooner had he disappeared than Peter was balancing on his head, cantering round, taking the jumps – still on his head – and keeping us all in fits of laughter, when in came the corporal at a fast gallop, screaming his head off, and tearing off his corporal's tunic, with the spurs insignia above the stripes which signified that he was a rough rider. "You! You!" he shouted to Peter, "You'd better wear this, you're a better bloody rider than me!" ' Needless to say, Peter was overseas on the next boat! In later years, Peter told me about his chequered career in the army – most entertaining!

To return to my introduction to my new village: we boys continued our tour of inspection of the barracks, and I was next shown some life-sized wooden horses, mounted on stands by various shapes of iron connecting rods. I could hardly wait to be bunked up on to these wooden beauties – I was told that when the troops rode them they were saddled and bridled up, but a bit of string for reins did for we boys. I was told to sit tight by my new friends, and they began to push from the rear. My wooden mount behaved perfectly, rocking back and forth with fluid grace. I sat it with ease – 'Push harder,' I cried, 'harder, harder!' They pushed so hard the base began to leave the ground.

'You'll do,' said my friends, 'now come and try this one, then we'll try the one over there.'

I could tell from their expressive faces that I could expect a different ride from my new mount and sure enough, after being lulled into thinking all was well, it dipped at the front, making me cling on like grim death and bumping my face on its hard wooden head in the process. The other trick horse was a bucking bronco, pure and simple. If you were pushed really hard, it was very difficult to master. Needless to say, during the school holidays we scotched many a hole in the seats of our pants, and became very proficient riders of the wooden horses.

None of we boys had any fear of horses, and when the bugle call, 'Come water your horses and give them some corn, or I'll make you wish you'd never been born,' sounded, we were often asked by some of the more timid soldiers to lead their charges out to the water troughs. This we gladly did for a copper or two, making sure we were not caught by the NCO's. One day the cook sergeant's son was kicked in the face, unfortunately breaking his jaw, so that put a stop to our watering half-broken horses.

We got to know when a new batch of horses was arriving at the railway station. This was always very exciting – a batch of several hundred would arrive, all completely wild; I think they came from the plains of Argentina. When they were all unloaded, they were herded, by superbly mounted members of the riding-school staff, out of the station and on to the road leading to the stables. Well, not the road exactly, as all main roads in this military village had a dirt track bordering the motor road, equal in width to the main road, and this was kept for horses only. Once the staff had driven the herd of wild horses on to this track, how they went! Talk about cowboys and indians! It was all done at a full gallop, and how they turned them into the barracks grounds I shall never know.

I often thought of those rough riders breaking in this wild bunch, but break them in they did. Quite often fifty or more of the horses would escape from their stables and run wild until rounded up a few at a time. I was return ing home one dark night from my gym session when I heard the sound of running horses coming down the hill behind me. I ran as fast as my legs would carry me, burst ing into the police station yard and quickly fastening the big iron gate, just in time to see the horses race by. I heard such an almighty crash, and climbed on to the gate to see what had happened. I saw that one or more of the horses had hit an oncoming lorry head on. I could hear the squeals of the poor horses and the shouting of the lorry crew and suddenly I felt very sick. One of the horses struggled to its feet and came running up to our gate, trying to get in. I shooed him off and he ran in the direction of the stables. My next thought was to get Dad or the constable to attend to the accident. I opened our back door and rushed in. Mother and Dad sat by the fire with the wireless ear-phones on, listening to 2LO or 5GB on our crystal set. They took one look at me and nearly fainted! Unbeknown to me, the injured horse had smothered me from head to foot with blood when he tried to get through our gate.

Father told me later that two horses had to be destroyed, and believe it or not, the great round iron bar that went across a lorry's radiator in those days, had been broken in two by the impact. I called at the veterinary stables to have a look at the horse that had smothered me with blood – poor old boy, he was cut all over, but the main source of bleeding was from a broken nose.

As I have said earlier, it was quite a common occurrence to see loose horses dashing about in our part of the village – quite scary in the dark. I remember going to the picture show one night, which was held twice a week in an ex-army hut – silent movies of course, 4d to go in and 2d worth of Sharpe's Super Cream Toffees. What a night out for 6d! We shouted and stamped, and had community singing during the breakdowns, which were rather frequent. We emerged hot and tired, very husky and often itching, as we had to sit on long forms covered with sacking and stuffed with straw, an ideal home for fleas. My friend Edgar and I made our way home in the dark, excitedly discussing the various films we had seen.

Part of our walk home was through what we called Government; this was a field separating the Royal Ordnance Stores from the barracks. In order to keep the general public to the footpath it was fenced in on both sides with iron railings at least seven feet high. We were half-way along this walkway when we heard loose horses coming full tilt towards us. We were very frightened as we felt sure we would be trampled to death – then I had a brain wave; I shouted, 'Run to the sharp bend, cling to the railings on the inside of the bend and they may miss us.' This we did for what seemed an age, feeling the horses rushing by us. It was terrifying, and when the last horse had passed I shouted to Edgar, 'Are you all right?'

'Yes,' came the reply, 'are you?'

'I just had a knock in the back,' I said, 'but I'm okay.'

That knock in the back turned out to be a kick I had received, and I had the impression of a horse's hoof in the small of my back for a long time, which resulted in my being examined by the army MO until I was eventually pronounced fit. I quite enjoyed my visits to the army sick bay as everyone made such a fuss of me. I bet some of the old sweats trying to pull the wool over the MO's eyes would not get such VIP treatment.

We arrived at our new village in the school summer holidays and this enabled me to get to know the layout of the three sections named Upper, Lower and Road, which made up the complete village. The school was in the lower section, almost opposite the church. There was an infants' school, a girls' school and a boys' school, all housed in separate buildings. The headmaster of the boys' school was a charming man, steeped in country life and also a very keen gardener. I liked him immediately I saw him. He must have had a good effect on other boys too, if the annual scholarship results were anything to go by. In those days there were so few scholarships to be won in the whole of the county, and it was a feather in the cap of a school to win one. You could tell what an achievement it was from the Roll of Honour displayed on the wall in the head's classroom. This was a beautifully made board, dating back, I imagine, to the year scholarships were first awarded. I can't remember a year that was a blank but I do remember that some years two names were added to the list. We had it drummed into us to work hard and to keep up the reputation of the school, and we were expected to get at least one name on the Honours List each year. Needless to say, my name was not added. However, I did, with another boy's help, please our keen gardening headmaster by winning second prize for a school garden plot, in a competition for the best garden in the whole county. Our prizes were a splendid gardening knife each, and I kept mine for nearly fifty years before losing it when on holiday.

Some of us did get in our kind old headmaster's bad books by bathing in the canal just behind the school playground. We did not realise that our feet were scraping the clay away from the bottom of the aquaduct, consequently letting the canal water run out on to the road beneath.

The church had a flying goose for a weather vane – most unusual. We were told an interesting story of many years ago, when the good people of the village were plagued by flocks and flocks of wild geese and were unable to grow any crops in field or garden as the geese just gobbled them up. Consequently, the people were very poor, and in desperation they went to the Abbot for help. He put a curse on the geese and they disappeared overnight, never to return, so I was told, as long as the goose weather vane flew over the church. How true this is I cannot say, but I do know I never saw a wild goose during the time I lived in the village, although there was plenty of marshy ground to attract them.

It was a nice church and very cosy, but the services were interrupted by the express trains which roared over the viaduct which was so close to the church. I remember one Sunday evening the Royal Scot, a night train pulled by two powerful passenger engines, making a dreadful noise and eventually coming to a standstill on the viaduct – apparently one of the huge driving wheels of the second engine had broken up, damaging signal boxes and station alike. The driver of the first engine was commended for good thinking – he kept his engine pulling hard, whilst the other driver applied the brakes on the train, thus preventing a derailment.

The rector was an outspoken Irishman with a very deep voice, an ex-military man, ideally suited for this parish. He would amuse us at village get-togethers by singing such rousing songs and had such a deep, powerful voice. He always ended the evening's entertainment, after lubricating his vocal chords with a well-known Irish gargle, with a rendering of his and our favourite song – 'Oh Father O'Flinn was the Best of Them All' – pleasing us with several encores.

I remember coming out of church one winter evening, unable to see a yard in front of me for thick fog – what a pea-souper! We all stood in the church porch, hardly daring to venture out, and my mother said to a regular evening church goer, a woman who was, unfortunately, blind, and lived in a lone house along the tow-path of the canal, 'How are you going to get home tonight?' I think we should come with you.'

'I shall be all right, my dear,' said the old lady. Someone remarked that she hadn't even got a lamp. She laughed and said, 'My dear, it makes no difference to me whether its foggy or moonlight, and what would be the good of a smelly old lamp? I am better off than you as I can find my way home so much better – thanks all the same.' For the very first time it was brought home to me that even a sunny evening was a complete black-out for a blind person.

There were times when I watched with bated breath the boisterous riding antics of the young officers, His Royal

Highness, Prince Henry, Duke of Gloucester, numbering among them. What happy, devil-may-care, young men they were, and Prince Henry was no exception. When his dog killed some of our hens he came to see Dad to say how sorry he was, 'Damn dog, how much do I owe,' etc. He made us feel so much at ease, I could hardly believe he was a Prince of the Realm, so nice, so charming and so ordinary.

I remember my father telling me that one day Prince Henry was on a train going to some big event, I don't know where, when the train began to slow down. The Prince looked out of the train window and, on seeing the bunting flying at the entrance to the town, said, 'Another circus, and I'm the bloody clown!' I liked that story.

One moonlit evening I heard such a din coming from the walnut plantation where the commandant's breeding sows were kept – they ran loose, rooting among the trees, keeping themselves, I would think, or nearly so. Squeals of protest were coming from the pigs, amid much laughter, and I saw, to my amazement, young officers in dress uniform, riding and attempting to ride these unwilling steeds. One officer, to the encouragement of his brother officers, was trying to ride a big old sow up the steps into the officers' mess. I knew it was a common occurrence to ride a horse into the dining-room, but the entry of an officer mounted on a pig, would, in my opinion, take some beating. I would imagine the commandant was away somewhere that night.

I remember the commandant having an enforced stay away from the mess one night – it is only with the passing of time that I dare tell you this story, and it came about like this: one evening there came a knock at our door and Mother and I opened it together – it was advisable when Father was out that we should both open the door as we often had odd people call, demanding to be locked up in the cells for the night, asking for food and shelter, and making all kinds of requests. Our stock answer was 'Come back later,' hoping they would go away. Quite often they would move on, but sometimes we would get an awkward customer who would kick the door, shouting and singing and most times, swearing, upsetting Mother and frightening me, until Father came home, when they would have their wish granted and be locked up for the night. However, on this occasion, two officers in evening dress greeted us with, 'Would it be possible to borrow the Sergeant's old tunic? We would only need it for an hour – we have a play on in the mess.' Mother was very dubious about this, and was just about to refuse this unusual request when the officers, whom I knew, winked at me. I immediately guessed that they were up to some well thought-out prank, and wishing I could be a party to their mischief, I persuaded Mother to relent. I ran upstairs and brought down an old tunic and helmet, and off they went. In less than an hour the uniform was returned to us with many thanks.

By now it was getting late, and Mother and I went to bed. In the morning when we were having our breakfast, Father came downstairs and sat by the fire having a cup of tea. He remarked on what a hell of a night he had had; some fool had arrested the commandant on some pretext or other and escorted him to sub-division headquarters, where he was taken to the charge room and asked to wait, whereupon the police officer had disappeared. The commandant sat impatiently waiting to be charged or whatever, when in walked the station sergeant. On seeing the commandant he asked, 'Can I help you, Sir?' The commandant, by now breathing fire and brimstone, retorted, 'You should know if you can help me or not – one of your lot brought me here, asked me to wait, and I haven't seen the bloody fool since!' The station sergeant couldn't make top or tail of this, but found a car to take the fuming detainee home. In the meantime, a search was organised for the 'bloody fool of a police officer', but he was never found. Mother and I, tongue in cheek, looked at one another, silently promising that we would never, ever tell Dad about those young devils who cadged the tunic for a play!!

Chapter 9

My Wings are Clipped: Caged in an Industrial Citadel

My life for the next two years was idyllic, getting my work done at school, no problems there, playing with my friends, and doing my share of the household chores. One of these I absolutely detested as I felt so much time and energy was wasted on this task – this was cleaning the cutlery until it shone like silver. This had to be done twice a week, and all to no avail as it was dull and stained by the very next day. Mother, being one of the old school, where cleanliness was next to Godliness, told me to clean the cutlery, and clean it I did. What a slow, uninteresting performance it was. You took an old bottle cork, dipped it into a brown powder called bath brick, then, resting the knife on the table, rubbed the powder-covered cork up and down the blade until both sides shone. After finishing the knives, it was the turn of the forks and spoons. I found it advantageous to dip the cork in a little water in order to make the powder cling, and if the water ran out or was spilt, I used spit! Hygiene be damned!

One day we visited our market town, and on going into Woolworths we saw, to our amazement, cutlery suspended in jars of vinegar, completely untarnished. Hooray! Stainless steel had arrived! I encouraged Mother to complete her labour-saving purchase of knives, forks and spoons, by investing in a small methylated-spirit burner for sixpence, with a special small kettle to fit, also costing sixpence. This she did, and we were able to enjoy a hot cup of early morning tea without having to light the fire to boil the kettle – luxury for only a shilling, and also ridding me of my hated chore for very little more.

I continued with my gym sessions, getting very fit indeed, and developing muscles I never knew I had. I grew like wildfire until I reached five foot ten inches at the age of fourteen, and there my growing stopped. This was a great disappointment to my mother, who came from such a tall family, and Dad said I would hardly make a policeman. I told them it was all the to-ing and fro-ing I had had to do, which had worn my legs away.

Our deputy headmaster formed a Scout troop. I was accepted into this as I was one of the tallest boys, and very soon became a patrol leader. I thoroughly enjoyed scouting – what an excellent training for a young lad on the verge of going out into the world. I found that so many of the skills gained whilst studying for various proficiency badges, i.e., first aid, signalling, knot-tying and splicing ropes, fieldcraft, artificial respiration, to name just a few, came in so useful in later life. I think I took the training so seriously that I never forgot a thing.

We were very proud of our headquarters which were situated at a beauty spot called Brockhall which, my wife tells me, means Brock's Hole. I can well believe this, as it was a spot where you would expect to see badgers. Our senior master was the Rev. Shackleton who was some relation to the Arctic explorer – he was a grand chap.

Even with several nights a week at the gym, plus Scouts on one night and Saturdays, I still found time to continue my long attachment to the barracks. It was so interesting watching the Army tradesmen at work, and although I may have been in the way sometimes, I was never asked to move. They showed such skill with the most basic of tools – the farrier, shoemaker, harnessmaker, tailor, carpenter, blacksmith, veterinary surgeon, etc., all did their jobs with ease. It was so obvious that, even under adverse conditions, the troops would never be let down by these efficient tradesmen.

When the time came for me to leave school my father told me that Captain Stubbs had offered me a job in the Royal Ordnance depot (known as the Stores). I was to be a civilian apprentice in the Royal Engineers and would be trained as an electrician. This pleased me a great deal as I knew so little about electricity, although I had realised it was the coming thing, and would, in time, be in every house giving light at the flick of a switch. But little did I know that it would almost rule our lives – when there is a breakdown nowadays in the supply lines, we are all at a loss. One old fellow I worked with said, 'Treat it with respect and it is a good friend, mess about with it and you make an enemy,' – I think I know what he meant.

I passed by the closed gates of the Stores almost every day on my way to and from school. I often spoke to the policeman on duty, trying at the same time to peep through the small door in one of the gates, but with no luck; my way was always barred. It seemed to me to be a very mysterious type of works, surrounded on all sides by a very tall, forbidding wall. There was only one entrance and this also served as an exit. Built next to the gate was a gatehouse, surmounted by a clock tower, which also housed a Church type of bell. The gatehouse was the police headquarters, built on a bridge under which went a canal. A portcullis was lowered from the gatehouse to block any entrance by boat, and a swivel road bridge had to be turned to let barges through. There were also two railway tracks through the main gates, and these were used by the Stores' engines only.

I began to wonder what it would be like to work in such a place. However, I would soon find out as I was to start work on the following Monday. I knew the bell started to ring at 6.55 am and finished on the stroke of 7.00 am, when the gates would be locked, turning away any late comers – no drifting to work at any old time. When Monday arrived, I beat the bell and was through the gate in good time. I reported to the guard room, where I filled in a register and was given a brass check disc with my number on. I was then shown where to file in and where to hang my disc in its proper place. I was told where to place all matches, cigarettes, etc., from my pockets, putting them in a recess under my disc. These instructions did not apply to me as I was a non-smoker. My belongings would then be secured until clocking-out time. I was instructed by the policeman who was putting me through this procedure that even if I didn't smoke, I was never to take matches in, as they could be very dangerous.

I was shown where to report and opened the door into a workshop full of lathes, drilling, grinding and cutting machines, each individually driven by a wide, flat leather belt, which in turn was being driven from an overhead shaft and pulley-wheel stretching the length of the workshop on both sides. What a hideous noise! Machines working, belts flapping, men shouting to make themselves heard and pointing to a small office, making me understand that that was where I must go.

I found the man I was to work under, a kindly looking man, an ex-sergeant. After a brief chat, I was told, more or less, what was expected of me. I was issued with a tool box containing, I was told, £40 worth of tools. When I signed for these, I was advised to keep them locked up, as any losses wold have to be put right by me. 'Now, young fellow,' my sergeant said, 'each morning you report to the police guard room, pick up a list with details of any bulbs that have gone out during the night, go to the stores, draw the required number of replacement bulbs, fit them and return the old bulbs to stores, so that the new ones can be accounted for. I will come with you for the first few days to show you round.'

I duly collected my list, reported back to my sergeant, and was given a short ladder to carry, then off we went. I was told I would have no trouble finding my way about because, with usual army thoroughness, every building was numbered 1, 2 or 3, etc., as the case might be, each section of that building would be lettered A, B or C, and so on, and each passage or aisle would also be numbered. For instance, if, on your list you had No.1 A 30, you looked for Building Block No. 1, found Section A and Passage 30, and you would soon find your faulty lamp.

Without any difficulty, I found my first dud bulb in a narrow gangway at least thirty feet above my head.

'There you are, son, up you go,' said my instructor.

'Where is the ladder kept?' I asked, glancing at my short ladder.

'We don't use ladders, we make use of the handles on these rifle boxes, so put your foot over the rope handle, your toe under the wooden handle, and you will soon see they are perfect for climbing.'

Without further ado, up he went with me following. I very soon became adept at climbing up rifle cases, always wearing boots with strong toe-caps.

What dull, uninteresting places those rifle stores were, with thousands upon thousands of boxes all looking alike, stacked so neatly right up to the roof, with narrow passages between. They were very dimly lit, and though it was easy to find your way in, it was rather hard to find your way out, and if you asked for help from the odd man you saw, he was, as a rule, not at all co-operative. I was shown the powder magazines, ten in all; half of these were dummies, built exactly the same. I was told I would soon discover which were which, and in the live ones I would be escorted everywhere. They were like giant, man-made caves, very claustrophobic – you felt cut off from the world, and always at the back of my mind was the fear of an explosion. Oh dear, I thought, if this lot goes up, I will be spread over half of the county.

I was expected to finish my morning round by 8.45 am, when the real work would begin, or so I was informed. Sure enough, a different type of work did begin. When my old sergeant found he could trust me, he said, 'Look, boy, we are going to work like the very devil, non-stop, so that we get our quota of work done by dinner-time. Keep quiet about it, grab your sandwich box, and meet me in the old transport shed.' This I did, and there in the shed I found a senior officer in earnest conversation with my sergeant, both of them peering at the engine of a car.

'We'll do our best, Sir,' said the sergeant. When the officer had gone, everything was explained to me. It seemed that all the officers liked the sergeant to have a look at their cars now and then, and he needed my help.

'Fine,' I said, 'but what about the Stores police?'

'Oh, I do theirs as well,' was the surprising answer. And that is how I received my first training as a motor mechanic.

There were other times when I would be told, 'Keep out of the way this afternoon and don't let the captain see you. If you are asked where I am, say you have lost me.' (To lose anyone in this vast, secretive complex was comparatively easy.) 'If I am wanted urgently, you know where to find me?'

'Yes,' I said, trying to keep an innocent look on my face, 'playing billiards in the police club room.' I loved these free afternoons – I could explore this place of mystery to my heart's content.

I found steps in odd places leading up to the top of the perimeter wall; I had not realised that the wall was so thick and the top so flat. It would have been possible to march a platoon of men along its entire length. Spaced out at intervals on ground level were gun emplacements, which could only have been built at some previous date. There were no apertures showing through to the outside, but it looked as if it would be quite a simple job, if it became necessary, to make slits for firing through. Standing on this parapet and looking around me, letting my boyish imagination have free rein, I could picture myself as a defender holding this fortress against the attacking hosts FORTRESS!! CITADEL!! ENCAMPMENT!! All of these titles seemed to me to fit this Government complex so much better than Ordnance Store. Anyway, I thought, as I pondered on the prison buildings, which looked older than the rifle stores, who would lock prisoners up within easy access of arms and ammunition? Could not this be the original barracks of yester-year, the home of a mobile army situated on crossroads going North, South, East and West, in the very centre of England, a lesson learned from the Romans? I liked to think I could be correct in my interpretation of my sombre place of work.

I wonder if the description 'sombre' for this work place was also felt by the two hundred or more men who worked there. I did not hear much laughter, and many times I was hauled over the coals for running to work – 'Run away from it, boy, not to it,' I was told. I noticed that this bit of advice was heartily endorsed by many of the men at clocking-off time – you had to be quick on your feet to avoid being knocked over in the rush.

When I reflect on this pattern of behaviour, shown by such decent men, so happy in their normal village life, then follow the industrial disputes of nowadays on the television, I can only think, after hearing both sides of the dispute, it is not the money, or the work, but work conditions, of which we are unaware, that are often the source of conflict.

I have always been independent, as far as possible, preferring to be my own boss. My mind was made up about this when I looked at the silver sixpence in the middle of my hand (I gave Mother the ten shillings of my weekly pay of 10/6d), after a five and a half day week at work, shut off from the outside world.

When my father told us that we were moving again, I thought, Hurray! I like the village, I like the army, but I don't like my work place! Next time, I promised myself, it doesn't matter what kind of job I do as long as it's in the open. It's nice to feel free.

After writing about the home, school and work place I left over sixty years ago, my wife and I decided to revisit this area on one of our car outings. What a change! The barracks is now an MOT testing centre, the police station is an antique centre, the officers' mess has disappeared completely and been replaced by a modern housing estate, the Ordnance Stores are unused and becoming derelict, and the three schools are overgrown and neglected, no longer echoing to the sound of childish laughter – all very depressing.

Chapter 10

To Have the Right to Choose Your Work, or to Have No Say in the Matter: How Important This is, As it Shapes Your Whole Adult Life

The truth of this was brought home to me when listening to both my grandfathers, each telling me at different times of their upbringing and childhood days. Both started work, and I mean work, at the age of seven. When I look at some of my young relatives playing so happily at childish games, with apparently not a care in the world, and ask, 'How old are you?' I sometimes get the answer, 'I am six,' or, 'I am seven,' and I shudder as I think of their great great grandfathers at that tender age, working all day and every day, from daylight to dark on the farm.

My mother's father started this true tale as follows:

'I was one of three brothers; my father was a keeper on a large estate in Buckinghamshire and we lived in a cottage in the woods, a long way from the nearest village. I was not a regular attendant at school; for one thing, it was a long way to walk to and from, and we sometimes had a job to find the penny we were expected to contribute towards our schooling every week. What with helping my father in his work, doing jobs for local farmers, and attending school at odd times, the time flew by, and in no time at all I was seven years old. Now seven was the age when you were no longer expected to attend school, and I went to one of the estate farms for a job, hoping to go crow minding, but not a bit of it – I was told to lead the horses of a plough team. The ploughman was a big, surly man, who shouted at me nearly all day long. It was no easy task, guiding those huge draught-horses, which towered over me, and with a toss of their heads almost lifted me off the ground. My boots became clogged with mud, and I hardly knew how to put one foot in front of the other. If I wavered from a straight line, the ploughman would pick up a clod of earth and throw it at me, making me shed many a silent tear. When the day's work was done, my mother would come to meet me, having to carry me home, tired out. I nearly always fell asleep cradled in her arms, waking up in our cottage when my father came home for his tea. After tea it would be bed, because 6 o'clock in the morning soon came round. That is how I started work, and so it went on from one job to another, one farm to another, liking the summers but hating the winters.

'My father and his brothers were all very big men, and we boys looked like being the same. I grew tall and broadened out until, at the age of eighteen, I was six foot three and a half inches in my socks, and weighed eighteen stone. I had been giving a lot of careful thought to my work on the farm, and one day I told my parents that I was going into Buckingham for a day or two. I walked the long way to Buckingham, reported to the old jail in the town centre, and asked if I could join the police – to cut a long story short, I passed all my tests and was accepted. I was now a member of Buckingham Police Force. My parents were delighted at my news, and wished me all the luck in the world. I remained in Buckingham for some years. I did feel, however, that the opportunities for promotion in such a small town force were very limited, and consequently applied for a transfer to Northamptonshire.

'Northamptonshire Police Force was, in my opinion, a more advanced, go-ahead establishment, and so it proved. Once my transfer had come through, and after I had been put through my paces in this new force, I was asked if I would join what I can only describe as a specially trained unit, designed to deal with disturbances of a violent nature. After giving the matter some careful thought, I felt I was big and strong enough to cope with the demanding nature of this special unit. I was also single and unattached, so I accepted the offer.'

My grandfather went on, 'You may think that in those far-off days, people were mostly down-trodden and well-behaved, but not a bit of it. Violence flared up at the least excuse, and sometimes without an excuse. For instance, we had to deal with what we called cow hocking. This was a beastly form of senseless cruelty. The poor animals in the fields would have their Achilles' tendons slashed, leaving them helpless and unable to get up, so that they had to be put out of their misery. The sadists who did this to poor dumb animals turned very violent when caught, and were often in gangs. Had they killed and eaten the animals you could have perhaps understood their motives, but no, they just maimed them. When they physically resisted arrest, we were not sorry.

'At the time I joined this mobile force, many of the railway lines and canals were being built. This work was done by huge gangs of men who lived hard, worked hard, and fought hard, mostly itinerant navvies. What battles we had when they were crazed with drink. I remember a very narrow escape I had from death during one of these disturbances. I was over-powered, tied to a wooden tar barrel, and set alight, to be rescued in the nick of time by my comrades.

'As the railway tracks advanced, so we advanced with them, setting up camp at different places. At one point, our camp was set up on the outskirts of Kilsby. We stayed there for a considerable time as the navvies had a formidable task in building Kilsby tunnel. On my off-duty days I went into Kilsby for supplies, and there I met a young schoolteacher and we became very friendly. I was invited to her home to meet her parents, and we soon became engaged to be married.

'After Kilsby tunnel was completed, the railway track had now reached Warwickshire, so we Northamptonshire fellows were sent home. I was made a sergeant and given a station of my own, with a house to go with it, and this is when I married your grandmother, my teacher. My teacher she was indeed, as under her careful guidance and tuition, I was able to make up for my lack of schooling, and was thus able to undertake several important and complicated cases. These brought me to the notice of my superiors, and I was gradually promoted, eventually becoming superintendent.'

'My word, Gramp,' I said, 'you did well to become a superintendent after leaving school at the age of seven.'

Boy-like, I asked him if, with all these rough encounters, he was ever frightened. My grandfather replied, 'The burning tar barrel incident frightened me, of course. I thought I was a goner! But the one thing that really scared me had nothing to do with rough-houses – it was so simple, but so unusual.' He went on: 'One moonlit night I was walking along a lonely country road, when I heard in the distance a rattling, clinking sound, coming towards me, unlike any noise I had ever heard before. It did not appear to come from one source but seemed extended for some distance, moving at a fast pace and getting closer by the minute. I hid in the hedgerow, trying to keep out of sight, when to my amazement, I saw the moonlight reflected from so many places, and all these glistening objects bobbing up and down at least six feet off the ground. Some I could see faintly and intermittently, and I wondered what on earth this monster could be. I heard the sound of so many thudding feet, muffled by the grass, coming towards me, and I waited with bated breath as this unusual spectacle drew nearer and nearer. At the very last moment, the penny dropped! The shining objects were sitting astride black horses! It was a sight I had never seen before – several troops of Household Cavalry in full dress uniform, the moon reflecting on their shining breast plates and helmets, their coloured plumes flying, the tips of their lances flashing the moon's beams all over the place, and their chains and harness jingling loudly – what a relief! I consoled myself with the thought – who would expect to see the Household Cavalry on a lonely country road on a moonlit night? Certainly not me!'

My grandfather also told me how he had had to administer the birch and cat-o'-nine-tails in the course of his duty. It distressed him considerably when birching young boys for what he considered quite minor, youthful misdemeanours. He went on to say that the magistrates of those days so often believed in the old maxim, spare the rod and spoil the child. However, he was quite often able to apply the birch (with his own boys in mind) with as little force as possible – in other words, he pulled his punches. But with the cat-o'-nine-tails it was a different matter, and in most cases this punishment was authorised for horrible crimes and cruelty perpetrated on animals and man alike – ghastly deeds, stopping just short of murder. My grandfather described the laid down procedure thus: the culprit was stripped to the waist and fastened to a framework, with arms outstretched and securely held, whilst the ordered number of lashes were applied to his back. A doctor would be in attendance, and when the punishment was over, salt would be rubbed into the wounds to avoid any infection. This treatment left a scar on the man's back for life. My grandfather thought this harsh treatment must have been effective, for he never saw or heard of a man who had been whipped with the cat-o'-nine-tails ever showing up for another dose. He had seen them in prison serving an ordinary sentence, but they had never sunk so low as to have the cat-o'-nine-tails administered again.

My paternal grandfather also started work on the farm at the age of seven. He, it would seem, was perfectly content with his lot, doing farm work practically all his life. I was able to tell, when we were both staying with his daughter (my aunt who had the smallholding and so loved her old pigs), that my grandfather loved the countryside and was steeped in country lore. Walks with him were a pleasure, and he opened my eyes to country signs and the mysterious ways of wildlife. I can smell the scent of the wild flowers that grew and flourished in the freshly reclaimed soil, to this day. The fields we walked over had been mined for iron-stone, and when the land was reclaimed I would think that wild flower seeds were brought to the surface which had lain dormant for years. They grew in such profusion, making up for lost time, no doubt, and the bees and honey-sucking insects were in their glory. I have never seen or heard so many skylarks singing their hearts out. I tried to find their nests, but was very seldom successful; the parent birds had very clever ways of enticing you away from their nests.

I had more luck with rabbits sitting in their forms, and I was shown how to recognise the tufts of grass that hid a rabbit, and how to catch it with my coat. I think my Gramp was an accomplished poacher, and I don't think his family went very short of food when they were small. He told me a funny tale, at least my grandchildren think it's funny when I repeat it to them – it went like this:

'One evening, when I was a young man, I had arranged to meet several other men in the village, as the moon was getting up, to make plans for a night's poaching. We stood in a group under the Cross Tree whispering our ideas to one another, but listening intently to these carefully drawn plans were two rather simple-minded boys. They wanted to come with us, but we knew this would not do – the keepers were not fools, and you needed all your wits about you. "No," we said, "you stay here and we'll bring something back for you."

'Little did we know that they chose to ignore this request and crept along after us. We put our snares down (we would call and examine these on our return), and moved with great stealth to where we knew pheasants roosted. By the light of a full moon they could be seen sleeping in a tall hedge, and it was quite a simple matter to catch them one by one with a loop on a long stick. To our horror, our simple-minded friends caught up with us. We shook our fists at them trying to make them go home and in so doing we woke an old owl in a tall tree above us. He looked down at us and in a loud voice called, "Who are you-oo?" Our unwanted followers, thinking it was the keeper, shouted at the top of their voices, "John Lowkes and Henry Dunkley, Sir!" bursting into tears and making enough noise to attract every keeper within miles. We all slipped quietly away, making a detour back home – not a very successful evening.'

Gramp also told me how, as a young man, he was very keen on a pretty young village girl, and he would smarten himself up and go calling on her. One day, when approaching her house, he could see her sitting by the window. He knocked on the door and the girl's mother answered it, saying, 'She's gone to Tompton (Northampton), laddie, she'll be back about nine o'clock,' dismissing the lovelorn young man for ever. When I look at an old photograph of Gramp as a young militia man in his smart uniform, sporting mutton-chop whiskers and a flower in his buttonhole, I wonder how anyone could have refused his overtures, but perhaps I'm biased.

The third member of our family to start work at the age of seven was my wife's grandfather. We were enjoying a drive in our car one day and admiring a perfect country scene on what is known to we locals as Danes Ridge, when I said to my mother-in-law, 'How well that farm stands,' and she replied, 'My father started work there as a little boy; he came from a village about ten miles away so he had to live in as a matter of course. I think he must have been fairly happy, for he stayed there for a number of years. Eventually he went to work for another farming family in the village where we still live. He told me what a lovely village it was before the building of the railway and marshalling yards – just a few pretty cottages and an odd farm or two, grouped around the church. Where the rows of modern terraced houses and shops are today were green fields sloping down to the river Cherwell. The river meandered at a leisurely pace, dividing our village from the adjoining hamlet – it was all so peaceful. This peace was shattered by the coming of the railway. However, this did bring prosperity to our tiny village community, enabling the farmer who employed my father to buy a large manor house nearby. When he vacated the old farmhouse, he offered it to my father to rent, an offer which my father gladly accepted. This was the opportunity he had been waiting for as he had a sweetheart named Ann who lived in a neighbouring village, so they were married as soon as possible and moved into the old house. By working hard they were able to start a smallholding. Father continued to work for his farmer boss, saving hard and eventually buying some land from him, together with the old farmhouse. We children were born there, and as soon as we were old enough we worked to help with the farm's expenses, I as a needlewoman and the others on the farm. My father bought a carriage and pair and several pony traps for letting out and hire. He also started a coal business. The earnings from this small farm, together with the business sidelines, enabled us to buy more land which we badly needed for our herd of cows.

'I went to work for a dressmaker in Banbury, and there I met and married a young solicitor's clerk. We lived in Banbury for some years, and four of our boys and one girl were born there. Unfortunately, my mother's health failed, and after she died we left Banbury to live at the farm and to keep house for my father and brother. This is how our six other children came to be born at the old farmhouse. I think Gramp enjoyed his large family of eleven grandchildren, for he lived to a ripe old age. In the course of events my brother also died, and the farm came to me.

'After the three oldest boys came back from the First World War, Charlie, not liking farming very much, went as an engineer on the railway; Harry, who was so gifted at art and had won an open scholarship to Birmingham as a boy, became a commercial artist; and Jack stayed and helped me run the farm, eventually taking charge of it, with the help of his younger brother, Bert.'

'Now,' I said to Mother-in-law, 'this is where I came on to the scene and became a member of your happy family by courting and marrying Joan.' Joan was the youngest but one of the eleven children and I met her quite by chance. I had stopped outside the farmhouse to speak to an older sister named Madge, when I spotted two charming girls, apparently waiting for her. I asked Madge who they were and she told me they were her sisters, Joan and Betty, whereupon she invited me to meet them. My heart turned over when I was introduced to the elder of the two – for me, it was love at first sight, and so it has remained throughout our married life.

When I became a full member of this large and happy family, I understood why Joan's Gramp and Granny had worked so long and hard to acquire the old house and land. At all times the house seemed alive with children, and there was always room in the attic bedrooms for more; a welcoming sight was the dining-room table, laden with food, often conjured up from I don't know where, and there was always someone or other who could play a tune on the piano, everyone in turn singing their favourite song. We all knew what song it was going to be, and joined in the chorus with zest. What happy times!

Nature, of course, took its toll: Joan's mother and father passed away and Jack took over the farm he had worked on all his life. We still kept together as a family, and when Jack became infirm and had difficulty in walking (a cow had slipped and rolled on him, crushing his hip bone joints), I called to have a chat more often than ever.

One day, when we were chatting, he told me how he missed his old cronies at the village pub, and how impossible it was for him to walk there. He also found it quite impossible to get into a car, and confided in me that having a drink at home was never quite the same.

'Jack,' I said, 'do you think you could sit on the tail-board of my old Land Rover if I let it down?' No sooner had I suggested this than he was struggling to his feet.

'Let's try,' he said. He asked me to back up to a nearby bank, then managed to sit down on the tail-board, handing me his crutches to put inside. 'Right James,' he said, 'don't spare the horses.'

How his old mates cheered to see him once again in the bar of the Fleur de Lys – he was a most popular man. We spent a very happy hour there, and when we arrived back home he thanked me and said, 'I didn't think I would ever have a pint in the Fleur again as long as I lived.'

It was a blessing we did make the effort, because not long afterwards he was taking his last ride, also in the old Land Rover, as we carried his ashes to be scattered on the hill that overlooked the farm and farmhouse so painstakingly bought by his grandfather and grandmother.

When we knew of Jack's request for his ashes to be scattered on the tall hillside, we all thought it a marvellous idea. When approached, the vicar agreed, saying, 'Why not? If that was his wish, I am quite willing.' And so, at the appointed time, Jack's two sons and their wives, together with his four grandchildren and the vicar, piled into the Land Rover, and off we set, climbing the steep hill to the top, our journey watched by Jack's cows through soft, dreamy, long-lashed eyes, knowing it was not milking time, and so pretending not to see us. The solemn family group stood bare-headed whilst saying a prayer for Jack, and his ashes were scattered by the vicar. Such a simple ceremony, so genuine and back to the earth.

On our way home down the hill, I said to the vicar, 'I'm sure Jack would like us to call at the Fleur as we go by.'

'I'm game,' said the vicar.

As we quietly filed into the pub, I said to Eric, the landlord, 'I have Jack's four grandchildren in the Land Rover.'

'Bring them in,' he said, 'they'll be all right. We have been watching you all from the bar windows, so we were able to say cheerio to Jack.'

Whilst we were having our drinks, and the children their crisps and lemonade, the vicar remarked, 'I remember the first time I came in here. I was with two colleagues, all of us dressed in mufti – we had come to look at the parish before I accepted the living. After we had had something to eat, I asked how far it was to Northampton, and this started an argument. Several said eighteen miles, some said sixteen and one, in a very loud voice insisted he could get there in under eleven miles. He was trying to prove he was right in no uncertain terms, when in walked the coalman, who ended the argument by saying, to the amusement of everyone, "My word, Francis, that's like shit from China, a bit far flung!" ' Such are some country parsons!

Chapter 11

A Village With a Thriving Cattle Market and a Giant Willow Tree for a Guardian

My first impression of my new village, Byfield, was very favourable. I am usually able to form an opinion at first glance as to whether I am going to like a place or not, and I knew immediately I was going to like my new home.

The stone-built police house was situated on sloping ground, protected from the cold winds at the rear by a very ancient hedge, growing on a steep bank. The front garden sloped gently down to a little-used narrow lane. Adjoining our house was a very pretty thatched cottage with small paned windows and a thatched porch, a fairy-tale of a house. I discovered that an elderly couple lived there, the husband being a very keen gardener, which was obvious from his flower-filled front garden and the beds bordering the cobbled path. He told me that both houses enjoyed the sun more or less all day long. The house, being on a bank, overlooked the five-ways crossroads, and this, in the days of very little traffic, could be very pleasant and entertaining. Between the house and crossroads was a giant of a willow tree whose graceful branches and delicate leaves made a silver curtain, breaking up the harsh outlines of the main road. When I remarked to the old gentleman next door about this huge willow tree and the way it leaned rather dangerously, he told me not to worry as it was going to be felled by the council. That was sixty years ago, and it still stands strong, proud and defiant, miraculously and completely filling in the huge aperture in its bowl with new and vigorous growth. This cave-like aperture made a shelter from the wind and rain for courting couples and people waiting for the bus alike, and it was also a favourite meeting place for the youth of the village. I think any modern day council would have a fight on their hands if they tried to slaughter this ancient giant.

Across the main road from our house was a very attractive village inn, the Rose and Crown, which was a long, stone-built building, thatched in a distinctive manner. To the rear of the inn was an attractive old malt-house, where the inn-keepers brewed their own beer in bygone days. Also, in the yard which adjoined the inn, was more than the usual number of stables and coach-houses. The reason for this was a cattle market, with all its cattle and sheep pens, market offices, and a weighbridge, etc., which was held to the front of the Rose and Crown. The farmers came from near and far, driving their sheep and cattle, with the help of their employees, to the weekly sale. Once their cattle were safely in their pens, they sent their men back to the farm to get on with the work, whilst they attended to the more serious side of their business, talking over a drink as they waited for the sale to commence.

The sending of the farm workers home was much approved of by the local unemployed men and boys, who would follow the sale with interest, buttonholing the new cattle owners almost as soon as their purchases were knocked down to them, with offers to drive their newly acquired stock home for a shilling or two.

The village really came to life on market days – two branch banks came for the day and kept open until 4 o'clock, and the pubs were also officially open for the same time. Unofficial closing times, perhaps, are best forgotten.

The village had learnt over the years to cater for the needs of country folk and farmers in particular. Our village boasted a harnessmaker, wheelwright, blacksmith, draper and tailor, shoemaker, a hardware store, two excellent grocers and bakehouses, a sawmill, a vet, and also a colt-breaker.

The colt-breaker had given up breaking-in horses just before I arrived in the village, due to an accident with an unbroken horse. The old men of the village talked of the accident as a very strange happening. Apparently, this lively, quick tempered colt-breaker had made an effigy of one of the current parliamentary candidates, over-emphasising the said candidate's gammy leg and hanging the completed effigy from the Cross Tree by its neck. He eventually cut it down, then burnt the straw-filled model on a bonfire, limping around the blaze as he mimicked the poor candidate with a stiff leg. This did not go down too well with many of the villagers, who said no good would come of it and that it was tempting providence. They nodded their heads knowingly when, shortly after the Cross Tree incident, the excitable colt-breaker was kicked very hard on his knee by a colt he was in the process of breaking, which resulted in his having to walk stiff-legged for the rest of his life. It was a great pity, as he was such a happy character and amused us all with tales of his youth, much of which was spent in driving a coach and horses. What a life he had led before his accident, and how very kind he was to twin mongol boys he fostered – the three of them were inseparable. I don't think the effigy incident was enacted with any real malice – just over-enthusiasm for politics.

One day, when talking to the old colt-breaker about the annual colt show due to be held in the village, I told him I had bought a piece of the colt show field, and that I was so surprised at the strength of the spring which welled up half-way down the field. He said that it was not really surprising, as when he first came to the village it ran out of the field and across the main road in front of the Rose and Crown, making quite a sizeable ford, and he had used it to wash his horses' feet many a time. He also asked me where I thought the water came from to wash down the cattle market – from my spring, of course. I would have liked to have seen the ford in its heyday; the picture from our house would have been complete, and it would have steadied down the traffic which races so uncaringly through the village nowadays.

What a wealth of country characters this village had, both young and old. I was fortunate enough to meet them in the old barn of a workshop I rented when I started a cycle-repairs shop. It had been a wheelwright's premises years before and still housed the foot-pedalled lathe he had used to turn wood. Because at one time it had been an old cottage, it had a huge ingle-nook fireplace, which was a great attraction for the village's out-of-work men and those too old to work. How they loved this old fireplace, around which at least ten of them could be seated on boxes and stools. They would collect firewood on their walks, and keep the fire going from morning until night in the cold weather – company for me and a haven for them. This was where I grew to know them so well as I listened to their tales of the past and present. They helped me with my cycles, collecting them and delivering them for me, and recommending me to their friends. I soon began to repair motor cycles, and the next step, it goes without saying, was motor cars, as farmers and tradesmen alike began to buy them.

The young out-of-work countrymen were so gifted with their hands, and after I had explained to them how to do a job, it was done with patience and thoroughness, leaving the tricky bits to me. All this for the price of shelter and the warmth of the fire.

I soon bought a very large car for hire and a station wagon with a folding hood, seating nine people (known as the dog-box), and trailer to fit on behind, and that is how I started my business. I remember seeing in the local paper some years afterwards, when a survey was being done of the village, my business described at length under the heading: 'From small acorns such oak trees grow.' I don't think it was an acorn, I think it was a fireplace in the right place during a period of terrible economic depression.

In our village lived a quietly spoken, unassuming son of the soil. Bent almost double by his labours, he could be seen walking unhurriedly to and from work, in rain, hail or shine, clutching in his hand what he described as, 'My old nag'. This was a short, stout walking stick, cut many a year ago from the hedgerow and polished by years of use – constant companions to one another. Even when pushing his old bike along, if asked by one of we young ones, 'Are you going to get on your bike now, Jim?' he would say, 'I'll think about it – I'm giving my old nag a ride at the moment,' and, sure enough, tied securely to the crossbar was his stout stick. He had another inseparable companion which he kept in his waistcoat pocket, the shortest clay pipe I have ever seen. Jim said it was for keeping his nose warm on frosty mornings.

This old nose-warmer of Jim Hodge's had a metal cap fitted on top of the bowl with holes in it, so that when the lid was closed, no spark could possibly be blown out by the wind. This was just as well, for Jim was a hay-tier. I must say, though, that Jim made it a practice never to smoke near ricks or buildings, a very wise precaution, meeting with the approval of many farmers on whose land he tied hay. One day I asked him why he didn't get another pipe, as Annie Batchelor had some in her shop and they were only a penny each.

'I've had pipes by the score, boy,' said Jim, 'not so long ago, every time you went in the pub for a pint, you helped yourself to a pipe from a mug standing on the bar. Baccy was only a penny a twist then.'

Jim went on to say that pipes with long stems wouldn't fit comfortably into his waistcoat pocket, and when he bent over to tie a truss of hay, they broke, but with this old pipe having no stem at all to speak of, it couldn't break. He had had it for years and, according to Jim, it was properly broken in by now, and smoked as sweet as a nut. It might have been sweet as a nut to Jim, but not to us.

Now, Jim worked for a gentleman who lived in Buckinghamshire, who had a business which supplied hay, more or less, all over the country. This gentleman and his family also owned the ironstone mines that had been worked in our parish for years, finding work for lots of interesting characters. Most of them had mined ironstone in other parts of the country and they fitted in well, bringing in new blood to the village and different ideas with gardening, etc. They played cricket well, among other things, and some had a thirst for adventure, setting off in the summer months, for several years running, to dredge gold in the frozen wastes of Canada – Kicking Horse Pass was so often mentioned. What tales they had to tell; when they came home they kept us spellbound.

Jim's Buckinghamshire boss owned the land mined for ironstone, and also several farms in the vicinity. This gave Jim a steady supply of ricks to be tied, and other farmers sold their ricks to his boss, so he was never idle.

One day Jim said to me, 'I hear you've bought a dog-box. What a pity you haven't a large trailer to go with it; if you had, you could cart my hay out of the fields to the railway station and load it for shipment elsewhere.'

'But I have got a trailer, Jim,' I said, and so started my association with Jim and his hay-tying for some time to come.

The very first day of my hay-carting I reported as told, and was instructed to load as many trusses as I could possibly get on with safety, rope them securely and take them down to the goods yard, where I would find a truck waiting for me and could ask the porters to help me unload. Jim told me how to stack the first trusses on my vehicle, showing me how to overlap the joints to make a firm load, and he then climbed back on to the hayrick and continued with his cutting. This was done with a very broad-bladed knife which had a handle set at an angle, almost in the shape of a figure seven. The hay is compressed in the rick by its own weight and lookes and smells very like flake tobacco.

I hurried to put my second row of trusses on, moaning and groaning as the thistles stuck in my hands. My hay-tying friend said I would be all right for the next three or four rows as I would lift them up with a pitchfork. I stuck the fork into the first truss – how I struggled and strained to pitch it up on to the load! Now, a truss of hay weighs sixty pounds if new and fifty-six pounds if old – imagine that on the end of a long fork. I did manage to get my first load on and down to the goods yard where a porter helped me to unload it, but I felt knocked up, telling myself I'd never be able to stand this – it would kill me.

When I returned to the rick, Jim was sitting down having a break, drinking nothing but cold spring water from a bottle. Apparently, when he was at work in the fields he drank nothing but water. After a time he asked me if I was ready for my next load.

'Jim,' I said, 'I feel so ashamed, but I don't think I can carry on with it – I'm whacked after one load.'

He gave a little chuckle and said he would help me put on the next load – he would do one side and I could do the other. I jumped at this, and in no time at all we had the first rows on.

Then the time came to use the dreaded pitchfork. I grunted and strained, the hay seeds sticking to my red, sweaty face, and the fork shaft bending with the weight of the truss. I peeped round the load to look at my partner, and to my amazement saw this bent old man, three times my age, forking the trusses up with no more effort than if he had pierced a new potato on his dinner fork.

'Jim,' I gasped, 'you've got me beaten.'

'I know, boy,' said Jim, 'I watched you with the first load – it was enough to burst your boiler. Why didn't you ask me for help? I've not been doing it for all these years without finding an easy way.'

I pondered for a time, then, 'I know, we both stick our forks in one truss and halve the weight.'

Jim laughed, 'My goodness, boy, if our boss saw two men lifting one truss, I would get the sack.' He went on, 'I'll show you how it's done – stick your fork in the centre of the truss as far as it will go, grasp the fork in one hand near to the tines, spread your other hand as far down the fork shaft as you can reach, pull with your top hand, push with your other, and as the truss comes up, stand the end of the shaft on the ground. The fork and truss are now upright – keep them upright all the time you are lifting them on to the wagon, and you will find it so easy, you will be able to keep on all day.' My first lesson from Jim.

When we were having our dinner break one day, I watched Jim drinking his cold water with obvious enjoyment, and asked him whether he had joined the Band of Hope or whether the Temperance Society had been after him. His reply was, 'I did once belong to the Band of Hope and wore my blue ribbon along with the rest of my mates. It was somewhere to go in the evenings when money was short. We had it drummed into us about the evils of drink, and were implored by our enthusiastic, well-meaning lecturers, to say to ourselves, "Get ye behind me Satan, get ye away." Also, as a further help, if ever we felt ourselves weakening, we were to talk to our conscience, as he was always with us to give us moral support. I have always been aware of conscience – he has pricked me on occasions, and on one particular day he came to my rescue. I had been working all day long up Red Hill, near to Rooks Spinney, tying a mouldy rick of hay in the blazing sun. It was one of those hot, sultry days, with thunder about – I was plastered with mould and seeds and everything stuck to me. How I longed for going-home time. At last I heard the church clock strike six and off I went homewards. As I walked down Banbury Road Hill, I saw that the White Lion was open, and old Joe Maycock was sitting on the form outside. "You look as if you could do with a pint, Jim," he said.

'My answer was this, "I could drink one down, Joe, if only to lay the dust."

'No sooner had I said this than conscience whispered in my ear, "No, Jim. Keep straight on, you'll soon be home." "Please conscience," I said, "just one," but conscience was firm. "No, Jim, keep on walking!"

'I got half-way up Banbury Lane, in sight of the Salvation Army Barracks, when a thought suddenly struck me. "Conscience," I said, "you're such a good fellow, I'll take you back and treat you!" '

How Jim chuckled to himself as he worked, after telling me this tale.

Sometimes in the evenings we young fellows would meet in the bar of the pub, which was quite close to Jim's cottage, for a game of darts, etc., and we could see Jim treating his conscience and, from all outward appearances, enjoying his treat. One evening, as the young do, we were arguing about some mathematical questions one of us had cut out of the puzzle page of a magazine, and we asked the landlord for some pencils and paper so that we could work these problems out. Jim said there was no need for that – just read them out to him. We read the questions out to him one by one, and we found that the almost instant answers Jim gave us were spot on when we checked with those on the back of the page. What had we here? A natural mathematician? We would do our best to find out.

One of the daily papers ran an article on maths, setting some very difficult problems to be solved, and giving the time each question should take. This enabled you to measure your IQ, as the answers were given in the paper the next day. When we read out these problems to Jim, the answer seemed to flow out, and when checked by next day's paper were found to be correct. What Jim might have achieved if he had only had the chance to develop and use this inborn computer of a brain, we shall never know.

Jim lived with his wife and daughter, Frances, in a typical thatched stone cottage which had a well in the garden. Frances, who I often see walking in the village, is about my age, and we often talk and laugh about the old days when we and our friends were forced by our parents to attend the Church Social Club whist drive and dance. This was held on Wednesday evenings, and we paid fourpence entrance fee. The MC made us dance with one another in an orderly manner around the room, and whoever you were partnering when the interval was announced, you took to the refreshment room, found a table for her, and treated her to a glass of lemonade and a bun, getting the same for yourself, at a cost of twopence each. Quite often your girl partner had more money than you, and would consequently slip you a copper or two with instructions to wait until the interval was nearly over, when the doughnuts would be going cheap – one bun was not much for a healthy country girl with an appetite to match.

Our dance band consisted of two elderly ladies from the village on piano and violin, both very musical (or so we thought), but so staid – how we longed for something to happen to liven things up. We didn't have to wait for long, for from across the Atlantic came the Charleston. Our dear musical ladies tried so hard to keep up with our gyrations, then when the Black Bottom was introduced, they were horrified – the Church Social had gone to the Devil!

There were occasions when some of we young fellows thought the Devil was not too far away, especially after the pubs were closed. Then the Social was invaded by our older brothers and friends, smelling of beer, their hair slicked back, and sweeping the frustrated housewives, who had so kindly been putting we young boys through the complicated steps of the Lancers and Quadrilles, etc., off their feet, and sometimes outside.

These social evenings were very much appreciated by the people from the outlying farms and, of them, the daughter from a hill farm, always turned up in very heavy hobnailed boots, ideal for her home environment, but frowned upon by the dance MC who asked her to don her dancing pumps at the door. What a healthy, happy girl she was, doing a man's job on the farm, and developing the muscles of a shot putter. We younger fellows very rarely asked her for a dance – we felt slightly ill at ease with her as she invariably took the man's role of leading, and you found yourself dancing backwards, with your right arm held up, and your waist tightly clutched by this young Amazon. When the more mature young men came in from the pubs, full of Dutch courage, she was soon whirled around the dance floor. I remember one evening after the dance was over, one of the more gentlemanly of the late-night crowd asked her if she would like him to walk home with her. His offer was accepted, and towards the lonely farm they made their way. When they reached the last gate, they stopped to say goodnight, and her escort found himself in a lover's embrace from which there was no escape. Scared to death, he asked to be let loose, with the excuse that he so badly wanted a cigarette. When he regained his freedom, he took out a much-treasured silver cigarette case, offering it to the girl, thinking a smoke might pacify her. To his amazement, she took his precious case and dropped it down the front of her ample bosom, never to be retrieved. What a way to lose a family treasure!

Chapter 12

As the Old Country Folk Say: 'Tis But Nature

The story of the lost cigarette case brought many a smile to knowing faces. One of the older single men assured us he would get it back, and we all knew he was more fitted for this act of bravery than any of we novices. He had joined the Yeomanry in 1913 as a volunteer, taking his own horse with him, together with lots of other farmers' sons. When war was declared they were called up and drafted into the regular army. Years after the end of the war, he still entertained us with tales of the French girls he had conquered, and he left nothing to our imagination as he recounted all the lurid details.

Whether he really was Jack the Lad, as he would have us believe, we rather doubted, but once he had said he would rescue the cigarette case, he could not back down. Now, we said, we will see if he really did know Mademoiselle from Armentiers. He had often bragged that he went with his officer to a 'house of delight' in France, ostensibly looking after the officer's horse, whilst the officer had dinner with Mademoiselle – leaving him plenty of time to ogle the chorus girls. (My word, we were told, they hadn't a stitch on!)

When the next Church Social dance night came round,

he asked the curvaceous custodian of the cigarette case whether she had still got it.

'Yes,' she answered, 'it's at home.'

'Bring it next week then,' said our French-trained Don Juan. The evening of the social dance arrived, and we watched the manoeuvres of the principal characters of this saga with bated breath, wishing them goodnight, a safe journey, and him a safe return, as they made their way homeward.

The next evening we all met on the cricket field, preparing the pitch for a match the next day, most of us pulling and pushing a huge iron horse roller backwards and forwards, until our elders and betters were satisfied the pitch was 'not bad'. We returned the roller to its rightful home under the old elm tree, then sat in a small circle on the grass (our betters had retired by now to the pavilion).

'Now,' we said to Jack, 'did you get it?'

'Yes,' was the reply, as he threw the case to its grateful owner.

'Tell us!' we all chorused.

'Well,' he began, 'when we reached the home gate, and we were having a kiss and a cuddle, I asked her if she was going to give it up to me or not, and she said, "You know where it is, next to my heart." '

Jack went on, 'I did no more, I plunged my hand, not down her bosom, as she expected, but from her knees upwards, exploring a few bits and pieces on the way. I soon had the case.'

'Go on,' we said.

'All I am going to say,' said our hero, 'he will be a lucky

chap who marries her – he'll never have to roam about at night like an old dog fox!'

'TWAS JUST NATURE!

There was, and still is, a small village not far from ours, where, in the opinion of most local people, existed a harsh and unfair ruling, imposed years ago by the titled family who owned the village, and for whom the cottagers worked. Fortunately, this ruling no longer exists. It was the custom, if a young single couple had a baby which came along before they were married, as babies sometimes do, for the boy and his family to be asked to leave their cottage home, and also the village. This did not apply to the girl.

We all thought that if this was justice, then this ruling should apply to the gentry as well, and if this had been so, we felt that many a mansion, or even a castle, would be empty and run down. Some of the more aggressive of us wondered if the squire who applied this rule was not afraid that some young ploughboy was usurping his so-called baronial privileges. 'TWAS NOT NATURAL.

One day when out walking and several miles from home, I met an older acquaintance and his girlfriend. She seemed such a nice girl of about his age, with beautifully coloured hair. She laughed and joined in the conversation, but all the time I felt she was not completely at her ease, and as she held on to her boyfriend's arm, seemed rather self-conscious, partly hiding behind him. Before wishing them good day and continuing my walk, the penny dropped, and in the words of one of our old village ladies, I judged her! Not to worry, I thought, they will make a good pair.

Some days afterwards, I met Ted (for that was his name),

and, with a twinkle in my eye, said, 'I say, old lad, what have you been up to?'

'I know,' he said, 'it was like this – close to the farm where she lives in is a clover field, shut up for mowing. We used to go into this field for a kiss and a cuddle; the clover was so tall, they couldn't see us from the farmhouse, and what with the heady smell of the clover, the scent of the wild flowers, and the droning of the bees on the honeysuckle, and the birds singing their hearts out, it was like being in heaven, and we do love one another.'

'Say no more,' I said, 'I quite understand, and so will the rest of the village.'

A month or two after this encounter, Ted came to me and asked if I would cart some bits and pieces of furniture for him as he had managed to get a small cottage in the village for only 1/6d a week rent. This I readily agreed to, so we picked up bits and bobs here and there, mostly gifts from relations and friends, and the little cottage looked quite snug after Ted's girl had told us where to put everything. When we had finished the furniture job, Ted invited me to the local for a glass of beer. When enjoying our well-earned drink, he said, 'I want to hire your dog-box to take us to the register office next Saturday.'

'Oh,' I said, thinking of the promising shape of his beloved, 'you're leaving it a bit late, aren't you?'

'No,' said Ted, 'we shall be all right.'

The happy couple were duly married on the Saturday, supported by friends and relations. I took my leave of them after they had cut the cake and we had all drunk their health.

On the Sunday morning following the wedding, I was going to early morning communion, when, to my surprise, I met Ted.

'My word,' I said, 'I didn't expect to see you up and out at seven o'clock in the morning after your wedding night.'

'I've been up some time,' replied Ted, looking rather sheepish, 'I've been and fetched the midwife, and now I'm going to get my mother.'

When I look at the happy, healthy grandchildren and great grandchildren of this loving couple, I wonder if, perhaps, at some time in the future, some path. lab. technicians, when examining a sample of their blood, might discover a substance they can't identify, and conclude that the only thing it compares with is clover pollen, honey from the wild bees, and a touch of honeysuckle. 'TWAS BUT NATURE!

Chapter 13

The Colt Show, Our Clockmaker, and the Dove House

The annual village Colt Show was looked forward to by most of the villagers; it brought a respite from their daily tasks and was of interest to most country people. A day or two before the event the field had to be made ready to receive the influx of horses of every kind and description. Jumps were erected, a show ring set up, farm wagons positioned for judges and spectators, and room had to be left for local tradespeople to exhibit and sell their stock-in-trade. Tents were put up for refreshments, smaller booths made ready for corn and cattle-feed merchants – there was always a glass of something to drink or a cup of tea offered when giving an order or paying a bill.

One very interesting character always attended these gatherings. He was a local village manufacturer of animal medicines and his green oil ointment was known and well thought of country wide. It cured all ills in livestock and farm workers alike and if anyone had a bad back, the old folk would say, 'You want some of Tommy Pettifer's green ointment – that'll do the trick,' and so it did. What was good enough for his horse was good enough for the man, better than doctors' medicines I've been told many a time.

In various quiet and lonely country spots gypsy caravans

would gather with their attendant string of horses, these to be sold or exchanged (all at a loss, if we were to believe them), on the day of the show.

When the great day arrived, farming families drove in from the neighbouring villages, often bringing horses they had bred or ponies their children had outgrown, all hoping for a bargain and vowing that this year they would not be deceived by the beguiling tongues of the gypies. I have heard how several customers, after visiting the Rose and Crown to meet their friends, have bought their own horses back from these bewitching dealers at an inflated price, not recognising them until they were turned loose and made their way to their usual stables. I was told in later years when I bought part of the show field that I would find endless golden guineas where this free and easy trading took place and where the dealers had lain on the bank in the sun, sleeping off the effects of the free drinks from the tents and the 'luck' money drink. Drunk they may have been, but they must have kept their hands on their money, for the only coin I ever found there was a George III penny.

The most fascinating part of the show for me was the parade of the various types of stallions, which came in all sizes and breeds, all looking so proud and defiant. Apart from the judging and prize giving, this parade enabled owners of breeding mares to make up their minds when selecting the most suitable mate for their mares, all the time bearing in mind the type of work required from the offspring of the union. How those proud, beribboned shire-horses arched their necks and held their plaited tails erect as they stamped their huge white-feathered feet, whinnying and snorting as they were put through their paces by their grooms. Such an almighty display of strength and latent power – I can only liken them to an express steam passenger engine standing in the station, gleaming and snorting, waiting for the off to race through the countryside at 100 mph, pulling its carriages and passengers with ease. I do wish my horse-loving granddaughters could have seen this equine display in the village they love.

This happy day ended at night with rides on the steam roundabout and swing boats, trying your hand at the coconut shy and eating sticky brandysnap, all this to the sound of discordant music and the splutter and smell of paraffin flair lamps.

The very popular Rose and Crown was kept by a charming family, consisting of husband and wife and three daughters. The father, the landlord, was most interested in horses and horse-racing, and the mother, a rather large lady, was very liberal in the use of face make-up, this at a time when making your face up was rather frowned upon by country women. Some of the more daring of them used just a touch of lipstick and I knew one who would rub her fingers on the lime-washed ceiling in order to 'powder' her face when going to a dance. I am inclined to think that the more the village women were shocked by the landlady's heavy make-up, the more she put on, and sometimes not very skilfully.

I can remember standing just inside the doorway of the village hall with a group of other young men one dance night, when in sailed the landlady, now known far and wide as the 'Painted Lady', who seized me and whisked me on to the dance floor for a waltz, leaving my friends grinning at the mis-matching of a young, slim boy, red-faced with embarrassment, and a six-foot woman, amply built and made up like a mature trouper of the stage. To my amazement she danced as light as a feather, and I quite enjoyed my old-time waltz. The music stopped and the call came to take our partners for the Lancers. I tried, as politely as possible, to make my escape, but all to no avail; a set was formed in no time at all, we bowed to one another (honouring our partners), and off we started. When we reached the set where you all swing together the men always tried to go faster and faster, eventually swinging the girls off their feet, showing their legs and lace to the seated spectators, who, with wolf-whistles and shouts of approval, encouraged them to go even faster. I wondered how I was going to get on with my mature partner? Would I get her off her feet, and if so, could I keep her up? I need not have worried, for as we whirled faster and faster, my feet were lifted off the floor and it was my turn to be shouting to be put down. We had encore after encore, and what with the heat of the fires and paraffin lamps and our exertions, we were all wet through with sweat; (one of my granddaughters tells me that only men and horses sweat, ladies perspire!) I glanced at my partner and saw to my amazement that all of her make-up had melted – black streaks of mascara ran down her cheeks, mixing with liberally applied rouge, and stains came from her hennaed hair – but my word, she was enjoying herself!

As I write about my painted dancing partner, the jovial landlady of the Rose and Crown, it is brought home to me how, in those far-off days, the people of the village were so dependent for their relaxation on the goings-on in the village inn. Many laughs were to be had, and stories told and listened to when men were working side by side in the fields and during meal breaks; escapades were repeated over and over again, losing very little in the telling and more often than not gaining in strength, with a bit added here and a little there.

I remember the old clockmaker who featured in these tales for many a year. His name was Crampy Dodd – the product of the joining together of two very old respected village families, the Cramps and the Dodds. This smooth-talking village clockmaker was not only an excellent maker and repairer of clocks and watches, he also made weather glasses (barometers). He had an understanding of events of nature and foretold fortunes etc. I suppose he could be compared in a way with Old Moore's Almanack – he insisted he could see into the future and foretold all kinds of happenings, some good and some not so good; they seemed to fit in with the mood he was in, and consequently the villagers tried their best to keep Mr Dodd happy lest some misfortune should fall upon them.

All this mumbo-jumbo put our clockmaker in a class far removed from the down-to-earth sons of the soil, who tended to give him a wide berth when indulging in rough horseplay in the village inns. However, with advancing years, Crampy Dodd, as he was known by everyone, began to imagine he had the gift to mesmerize man and beast alike. The more adventurous customers of the Rose and Crown, whilst keeping well out of the way of Crampy's hypnotic hand waving and the direct gleam of his staring eyes, plucked up enough courage to offer their dogs for the 'treatment' – 'Here you are, Crampy, mesmerize my old dog.' When no ill effect seemed apparent on their old dogs –

indeed, several of the dogs took offence at being treated in such a manner, and Crampy Dodd had to be rescued from their fierce jaws – the owners gained confidence, saying, 'If he can't put my old dog under his influence, he can't put me.' The boldest of them, winking at his friends, volunteered to be mesmerized, and as they stood in a circle round him, the mesmerist, with many strange passes of the hands and fierce glares from the unblinking eyes, muttered a few incantations at the unbeliever, whereupon he showed signs of being overcome. The eyes began to close, the man swayed back and forth, then with a loud moan, he sank to the floor, unconscious.

'He's out!' said Crampy.

'He's dead!' said the audience, kneeling down and putting their ears to the poor man's mouth.

'He wants a whisky,' said one;

'No, it was a pint,' said another.

'It will have to be brandy,' chorused the others. Mr Crampy Dodd willingly paid for all these drinks – he had underestimated his powers, and he didn't want the poor man to die! Gradually, the unconscious man began to come round, opening one eye and again asking for a pint. His mates chafed his hands and stroked his head, meanwhile helping him to drink his medicine, all taking sips, whilst crying, 'More, more, he's slipping off again – don't let him die!' Was there ever such a thirsty 'corpse'?

This little saga was enacted about once a week for many years, with the participants agreeing not to overdo things. My father, the village police sergeant, on entering the inn whilst on duty, was immediately rendered unconscious by our wizard, but because of an appointment was revived by only one pint of beer. Had matters not been so urgent, I am sure one pint would have failed to bring him round.

Our mesmerist gained so much confidence with so many successes that he began to brag that he could not be hung, and here we could have had a tragedy on our hands. One day, a nasty type of farmer, well into his cups, did no more than stand poor old Crampy on a stool, then taking some pigging cord from his pocket, put a noose around his neck, tying the other end to a hook in a beam. The poor old man fell off the stool and was left choking to death. An old man who worked for me told me how he cut Crampy down just in time. I know our foolish farmer was very severely reprimanded by one and all. What tales these old pubs could tell.

I found out a bit more about the Rose and Crown when I was given the job of census officer for the village. This meant going to every house and cottage delivering the forms with instructions on how to fill them up ready for collection in a week's time. Needless to say, I had to fill in at least half of the old peoples' forms – they always had the same excuse – 'I can't find my specs.' Bless them, what characters they were. How beautifully they explained differences in surnames, and what treasures were to be found in those old cottages. There may have been Hudson's cake sacks on the beaten mud floors but houses and occupants were spotlessly clean.

Outside one cottage I heard such harmonious singing by two male voices that I stood and listened for a few minutes before I knocked at the door, hoping to be asked in, and sure enough, I was told to 'come in'. Two old men sat in the chimney corner, one rather unkempt but the other very dapper, with his white starched collar and shirt-front. He also wore a tie – most unusual!

'Come in, my boy,' said the well-dressed one, who I knew as Alf Brightwell. His companion was Danny Douglas. 'We have filled in your form,' and to my surprise I saw that the form had been filled up in the most beautiful copper-plate writing. 'You found your glasses then, Alf?' I said, giving him a further glance.

'Yes, my boy,' and he went on to talk about himself. 'I had a good up-bringing. My ancestors were farmers and we owned the Rose and Crown. We grew our own barley and oats, manufactured our own malt and brewed our own beer which we sold for a penny a quart.'

Mr Brightwell lived to be well over ninety – a good advertisement for beer at one penny a quart. He put his well-being down to having a good breakfast and plenty of hard work. What a happy, ill-assorted pair he and Danny were. Mr Brightwell had two brothers, one who lived in Canada and one who lived in Daventry. The Daventry brother was our local collector of taxes, visiting farms and businesses to collect their income tax (these were the days before PAYE). This could not have been an easy task as very few people kept accounts. He must have been a diplomat to have squeezed money out of hard-headed farmers, who were notorious for pleading poverty, telling all and sundry how they had been losing money for years. An old farm worker who helped me always said, 'They must have had a lot to start with!'

I remember Mr Brightwell once stopped my father in the street, saying, 'Sergeant, you owe me a half-a-crown,' (2/6d, or twelve and a half pence nowadays).

My father reluctantly found the half-a-crown, saying, 'I'm blessed if I understand this income tax.'

'Neither do I,' said His Majesty's collector of taxes, always the diplomat.

The village benefited greatly from this Mr Brightwell, as he bequeathed the field known as the Dove'us as a playing field for the children of the village. This has been a great boon and a Brightwell Trust was formed which built a village hall at the top of the sloping field. The rest of the field, after being levelled, was turned into a sports complex and children's play area, with facilities for everyone.

When I heard the name 'Dove'us', I immediately thought of 'Dove House', and concluded that there must have been a monastery there in the past. I looked around and discovered a disused, filled-in pool where fish could have been kept. My supposition was confirmed when, during the ground-levelling, a most beautiful well was unearthed, very well built with cut stone so nicely fitted that this could not have been an ordinary village well. I am sure that this is the site of the Hospice of St John, recorded in a document dated 1313, probably a hospital for lepers and other such invalids and outcasts, who would be looked after by the good monks. It's nice to know that happy children run free where once this grim hospice stood.

Under the guidance of an energetic and foresighted parish council chairman, namely John Russell, more fields have been acquired adjoining the Brightwell field, including the old South Midland Junction railway station and yard. New trees have been planted around an area reserved for an extension to the old churchyard. Seats will be sited on this spot, overlooking the fields, spinney and hills, and it is to be hoped that both the dead and those that mourn may find peace and tranquillity there.

I wonder if this new burial ground will have any unusual headstones similar to some of those in the old churchyard, two of which are inscribed as follows:

> Thomas Thornton 1833–74
> All you that do behold my stone
> O think how quickly I was gone.
> Death does not always a warning give
> Therefore be careful how you live.

Another:

> John Austin 1851 aged 44.
> Robert 1873 aged 63.
> Time was I stood as thou dost now
> And viewed the dead as thou dost me.
> Ere long thou'll lie as low as I
> And others stand to look on thee.

Chapter 14

Our Jovial Family of Bakers, an Unusual 350-Year-Old Land Letting, and the Elephant Man

Every time we visited my long-lived uncle, he inevitably said before we left, 'How I loved your mother's Yorkshire pudding – it was just as nice when eaten cold. No one could make a Yorkshire like Nance – I wish she was here now to make one.'

Although Mother may have had a secret Yorkshire pudding recipe, I think her success was due to the fact that we took it to the bakehouse. I can remember to this day the people coming out of their houses and making their way to the bakehouse on Sunday mornings, carrying long, flat pudding tins covered with a tea-towel, and taking great care not to spill the batter. Some took their batter in milk cans and tipped it into the pudding tin on arrival at the bakehouse. Some were ashamed of their small or cheap joint of meat and did not uncover it until the last moment. In some cases the families were so large that they had two tins, one containing the meat and pudding, the other just pudding. It mattered not a jot to our baker and his sons; they knew exactly where to put each and every tin in the huge oven, and to whom each tin belonged – how I do not know – and if two customers claimed the same dinner, the baker soon sorted things out before a quarrel flared up.

When we formed a queue to collect our dinners, it was quite a social gathering, with everyone talking and waiting expectantly for the dinner of the week. At last the oven door was opened to the sound of hot, spitting fat and the tempting, mouth-watering smell of roast meat and Yorkshire pudding wafted over us all. Our dinners were taken out of the oven in the right drawing order, nearly always corresponding to your position in the queue. If anyone had nipped into the pub for a 'quick one', and failed to be in his proper place at the right time, he was jollied along and told to hurry up by the hungry crowd. I have known people to slip in bad weather, spilling some of their dinner, to the enjoyment of Baker Smith's hens. If this happened on the way to the bakehouse it was not too bad, the meat could be washed and the baker's sons or their mother would soon whip up some more batter, but if it was on the way home, it was a catastrophe and one which often happened to children who had been sent in a hurry because Dad was late back from the allotment or the pub, or both.

The dinner was always so hot I wore gloves winter and summer alike, as the traditional tea-cloth was hardly long enough to protect your hands. I would often ask my mother for an old towel instead, but no, it had to be a spotlessly white tea-cloth each and every week.

Baker Alf Smith was a jovial man, very rotund, with white hair and moustache, both made whiter by the dust from the flour; he had apple-red cheeks and very dark, twinkling eyes. His sons, Alf and George, were of exactly the same build and a happy disposition, always ready, at the drop of a hat, to burst into song. Mrs Smith was built in the same mould as her three menfolk, and Alice, the only daughter, whilst resembling her father, was of slimmer build – a nice, friendly girl.

No concert or social gathering in the village was complete without the Smith family taking a leading role in the entertainment of the crowd. I can remember to this day most of the songs and ballads Baker Smith sang at our Harvest and Pig Club dinners etc. One we always shouted for, as he was carving the huge joints of succulent hot meat rushed up by his family from the bakehouse, was 'Saw a little bit off the top for me, for me,' and our master baker would burst into song as he carved huge slices of the red, piping hot meat, to be put on the plates and passed around the long tables:

> Saw a little bit off the top for me, for me,
> Saw a little bit off the top for me, for me,
> Saw me off a yard or two, I'll tell you when to stop,
> All I want is a little bit off the top.

This went on for verse after verse, the chorus being sung with great enjoyment by one and all.

As the beer flowed and the good food – all home grown – disappeared into hungry tummies, how the gathering roared with approval as they joined in the singing led by the Master of Ceremonies, our baker, assisted by his family. Alas, we will never see the like again.

After the passing of many years, our baking family *did* get some Christmas dinners mixed, one of them being ours. It was like this: the baker was a good customer of mine for coke to heat his ovens, and when our son and daughter took our Christmas dinner to the bakehouse, I took a bottle of whisky along as a little thank-you present. The baker and sons, who had had a very busy and tiring few days before Christmas, and had started work very early that morning, emptied their tea mugs of dregs and filled them up with neat whisky. We left, saying, 'See you at one o'clock, Alf,' knowing full well that our dinner would be ready on time. When we returned to collect our turkey in its brand new outsized baking tin – my wife had spotted these old-fashioned tins in Russell's shop, and had bought one for her sister, Doris, who lived on a farm two miles away – whilst waiting for our golden brown, done-to-a-turn turkey to be taken from the oven, one person in the queue remarked, 'I don't know what old Alf and the boys have been up to, but they do seem a bit flustered.' And flustered they were! Our dinner was produced with a flourish by George, the younger son, and we grabbed it, hurrying home to my wife and Father and Mother. We placed the turkey on the table, everyone waiting expectantly as I prepared to carve, when the door burst open and in came our brother-in-law, who had collected his Christmas dinner half an hour before us, saying, 'You've got the wrong dinner, this is yours,' dumping down an identical turkey in an identical tin – the only difference being that our rightful dinner, after a journey of five miles, including an argument at the bakehouse, was, to say the least, cooling off! If there is a moral to be learned from this, it must be – don't present our baker and sons with a bottle of Scotch on a very busy Christmas morning! Still, it was a nice thought.

When the call came to serve her King and Country, Alice, our baker's daughter, joined the ATS. She was quickly put into the Catering Corps and was in charge of, and partaking in, the cooking of meals for hundreds of troops at a time.

She once said to me, 'I don't know how we did it, but we did!' A far cry from our village bakehouse, but her family training stood her in good stead. Well done, Alice!!

Baker Smith was a leading and energetic committee member of most of the village clubs and organizations. As we sat under the ancient Cross Tree in the evenings, we would see him emerge from his bakehouse yard carrying a briefcase, and we would enquire 'Where is it tonight, Alf?' The answer would be the Pig Club, or the Cricket Club, or maybe it would be the Thrift Club or Village Hall. We knew Monday night was Buff night, and we never had to ask when Land Letting was to be held as there was too much laughter and enjoyment to be had at this unusual ceremony for us to miss it.

It is a most unusual method of letting land, and has been going on in the village for at least 350 years. Every year about Easter time a round table is set up in the club room of one of the three village inns, and farmers and other interested people desirous of extra acreage of grass-keeping, gather. The restrictions and requirements are read out by the Chairman of the Land-Letting Committee, reminding one and all, and especially the people who were successful with the bidding, what would be required of them. Perhaps I ought to tell you more about the two fields to be let.

The Causeway was the larger field of the two and the rent money went, as the name implies, to the repairing and upkeep of paths in the village, clearly laid out in the following abbreviated copy of an ancient deed:

'I, Thomas Shaw, of this Parish, by deed dated the sixth day of January in the thirteenth year of the reign of King Henry VIII (1522) give a message and appurtenance in this

Parish to repair the common ways of this Parish and for other charitable uses thereto.'

The other field, Poor's Piece, was allotted by the Commissioners of Enclosure, the income to be used for the poor of the parish at Christmas time. Until the 1960s, this bought about six hundredweight of coal for about sixty poor or aged villagers, which was very acceptable at that time of year.

I will try and tell you why the unusual method of auctioning caused such fun for everyone. Through all the years I have known the ceremony, the auctioneer has always been a jovial village character, loud of voice, with a good sense of fun and a good capacity for beer, both drinking it and retaining it. His duty was to stand with his fingers in the centre of the round table and ask for a bid, and should someone in the crowd bid £20, around the table would march our auctioneer, saying, '£20 once'. On completing the second circuit, he would say, '£20 twice,' and on the third and last round would cry, '£20 for the third and last time'. If he received no other bid, it was his job to march sedately to the door, and if he could pass through it and close it after him, that bid held. But no, the bid was much too low, our gallant auctioneer was still in good voice, and the night still young. Someone would bid £21 and back would come the auctioneer to complete his round the table walk again. Bids would come in thick and fast, never allowing him to close the door – he would often have to take a drink to clear his voice, so you can imagine, with the frequent refreshment and the dizzy trips around the table, how very entertaining he became! When at last he began to wilt, the serious bidding would start, enabling him to close the door on the last bid and make his escape for a well-earned rest. In about half an hour back he would have to come in order to auction the second field.

The village poor and elderly benefited from this lively evening, and the village paths were repaired and weeded. We had so many bequests and money left for individual good causes which meant so much to the needy when first bequeathed, but as the years rolled by and inflation became rampant they realised so little money that it was impossible to administer them, so they were handed over to the Charity Commissions and administered as a whole.

I remember one little old cottage known as Bread Cottage, which had to supply a number of loaves of bread once a year for the needy, in lieu of rent. This was redeemed when two retired schoolteachers bought the cottage and pulled it down many years ago. A kind thought at the time, but who could keep a cottage in repair for, say, forty loaves of bread.

I recall being dressed down in no uncertain manner by the village bobby (my father), over about thirty doughnuts. It was the practice of myself and two friends to go down to the bakehouse very late on a Saturday night to see what delicious cakes and buns had been left unsold and to try and buy them cheaply by bargaining. On this particular night all we were able to acquire was a huge bag of doughnuts. When they were taken out of the boiling oil in which they were cooked (it was a delight to see them bobbing up and down whilst cooking), they were so fluffy and light with their jam centres, but when cold and stale, it was a different matter, and after eating three or four, they began to sit heavily on youthful tummies.

How should we dispose of them? None of our friends were too keen to help us out. As we walked along the street, we reached Mr Crampy Dodd's house. He had been married that day, leaving it very late in life before making up his mind to take a bride. As young boys do, we leered at his windows, wondering if she was under his spell, when we noticed that his bedroom window was fully open. What better place to get rid of our soggy doughnuts than through the open window of the love nest? We threw them in as fast as we could, bombarding poor old Crampy and his bride, when, to our dismay, the law descended upon us! My word, if modern youth could receive the dressing down that we had from the village policeman, times might be better. I also had a further telling off the following morning. Poor old Crampy – what a way to start a honey-moon.

What tales must have been told over the centuries under the spreading arms of the Cross Tree. Sitting one evening at our usual gathering place under this gnarled old tree, I listened to an old man named Walter Steel. He told us a tale that was hard to believe about a man known as the Elephant Man, and how he had driven him in a closed carriage with drawn blinds, through our village to a farm upon Red Hill. Apparently the Elephant Man was a poor, unfortunate creature with a very mild and shy personality, who had the terrible misfortune to be horribly misshapen of head and face. Walter described him as having a head as far round as the average man's waist, a nose that hung down like a small elephant's trunk, and very large ears. To make matters worse, he had a misshapen back which caused him to walk with a limp. We thought Walter was pulling our legs, but no, other old men confirmed that what he said was true.

It would seem that this poor creature had been put into a freak show in London, to be looked upon and reviled by the crowds who paid money to see him. After a number of years of this harsh treatment, he was rescued by an enlightened doctor who discovered he was not an imbecile but an intelligent human being, undergoing great suffering from the ridicule heaped upon him. The good doctor took him away from his squalid surroundings and installed him in two rooms of his own in a hospital. Under the care and kindness of this new treatment, the Elephant Man revealed his name as John Merrick. He was now able to converse with people, read books and write letters, something which had not been at all possible in the conditions in which he had previously been kept. Many people of good intent visited Merrick, among them Lady Knightley of Fawsley, the family who were one-time owners of much of our village and surrounding villages.

Lady Knightley arranged for Merrick to spend some time on the Fawsley estate, and an estate worker and his wife agreed to take him into their cottage. But the wife, on seeing poor Merrick (perhaps she had not been full prepared), fled, shrieking, into the woods. Now this is where Walter Steel, who worked as a boy for the Knightleys, came in. He was told to drive Merrick to a farmhouse at Red Hill, kept by a kind and compassionate farmer and his wife, who made Merrick most welcome. Red Hill is most beautifully situated, overlooking miles of open land and bordering on a large wood, densely carpeted with masses of bluebells and other wild flowers, with wild life in abundance. What a change for Merrick from the peep shows he had endured in such sordid surroundings. The woods were fully enclosed and shut to the public. Walter told us that Merrick hardly ever left this idyllic spot where he was so happy for the first time in his life. I don't know the ending to this tale but Walter said that Merrick eventually returned to London, and that was the last he heard of him. Quite a moving story for his listeners.

Chapter 15

'Light-en-it?' Our Village Doctor, and a Visitor from Canada

Our village, like many other villages of this period, had some likeable and unusual characters. I am sure they took pleasure in being rather odd. One of the oddest expressions used by the older inhabitants of the village whenever they met was, 'Light-en-it?' If it was pouring with rain and they were soaked to the skin, not one word of complaint would be uttered when you met them, just 'Light-en-it?' It mattered not how adverse the conditions were, or what unpleasant task was in hand, all would be expressed by this cryptic remark, made with such a straight face –'Light-en-it?'

One villager who was a First World War veteran and had seen a lot of heavy and bloody fighting (he received a very serious head wound towards the end of the war and had to wear a silver plate in his head for the rest of his life), told me how, after a period of heavy shelling their trenches were badly knocked about and his unit was ordered out one night to enable the Pioneers to repair and make good the damage. Early on the following morning, his unit was reluctantly returning to their advanced trenches when they met the Pioneers coming out after their night's work.

'Who do you think I saw?' he said. 'I saw old Crack Allen

trudging along, pipe in mouth, shovel over his shoulder, wet through and plastered with mud. How pleased I was to see a man from our village, the first man from home I had seen for years. I shouted, "Hello, Crack!" hoping that, in passing, we might exchange some home news, to which Crack replied, "Light-en-it?" and trudged on. I never saw him again until the end of the war.'

Another character, old Billy Bowden, was our versatile mole, rat and rabbit catcher. You name it, and if it moved, Billy Bowden would catch it. I have seen him laden with rabbits carried on a pole over one shoulder and he always had haversacks strapped to his back, bulging with I don't know what. He carried his ferrets in a wooden box slung over his other shoulder. He always had a short clay pipe in his mouth and wore a moleskin waistcoat and leather pads strapped on to his knees. He could be seen returning home in the dusk, after a very successful day rabbiting, with a little terrier dog trotting at his heels.

Believe it or not, farmers paid to have their fields cleared of rabbits years ago. Billy would never tell you where he had been and, if asked, would say he had been doing a job for the boss, although I can't remember Billy having a boss in those days. I think he had a dread of poachers usurping his best hunting grounds – I know poachers were very much in his thoughts and he often told me about sheep stealing, and how one man was hung for stealing a sheep from the Catesby gated road. He also told me how two of our village men were deported to Australia for the same offence, one several years after the other. Rumour has it that when the second man was being conveyed in chains in a boat up the river to his Australian prison, he met another boat coming downstream laden with prisoners returning from the prison camp, and in it was the man he knew from our village. He is supposed to have shouted, 'I'm going to do my stretch,' to which the other replied, 'I've done mine.' I would prefer to think that if they were true members of our village community, the greeting between these two unfortunates, as they passed one another in those strange parts of our colony on the other side of the world, would have been, 'Light-en-it?'

Our beloved village doctor, Dr Hope, was very well-versed in the idiosyncrasies of his patients. He laughed at their fears and quaint beliefs and expressions, and this made everyone feel at ease with him. They knew they could trust him implicitly – he was a friend of the family. This happy relationship between doctor and patient was a very good thing for the people of the parish at a time when not all stamped their cards or, indeed, had their cards stamped for them. I have known workers dismissed from their place of employment because their boss could not afford the few coppers for a stamp. I have had excellent workmen ask me to find them work, offering to work wage free, if only I would stamp their cards. Stamps in those days were one shilling and ten pence a week (about ninepence in present day money). I am ashamed to say I also could not afford to do this. Before the coming of the National Health Service, if you did not belong to a voluntary contribution scheme such as The Ancient Order of Buffaloes or Odd Fellows, etc., or join a Sick and Divvy Club run by the pubs, you could not, or dare not, afford to be ill enough to call in the doctor. Luckily, this did not apply to the villagers in our parish – they went to their family friend, Dr Hope, for advice, knowing full well that if he thought they were unable to afford his treatment, he would never ask for money. This was a good thing in my opinion as it allowed the doctor to treat you with his simple medical remedies before your condition became more serious. (Antibiotics had not been discovered then.)

The villagers tried to help themselves by contributing to the village Nursing Scheme. This was run on a voluntary basis, helped by the parish. Also, if you joined the Penny in the Pound Scheme – if you earned thirty shillings a week you paid one and a half pence a week, and if you should be fortunate enough to earn more, so you paid in accordance – this enabled you to have an ambulance to take you to Rugby Hospital free of charge.

Needless to say, with all this benevolent treatment, our beloved doctor did not die a rich man. After he passed away, the practice was bought by a young, up-and-coming GP, who attempted to collect the money owing to the practice. The Post Office had to make special deliveries with the bills of years, some twenty years or more overdue – they were in their hundreds, many addressed to people long since dead.

I have been told that when Dr Hope first came to our village as a young man, his only means of transport for the first year or two was by horse and trap or by a fast trotting young horse and gig, and his groom and driver was a young man by the name of Frank Brown. The young doctor, trying to keep up with the times, later acquired a motor cycle and side-car. It was a belt-driven Douglas motor cycle with an open wickerwork side-car, very reminiscent of the bath chairs of that period, affording very little protection from inclement weather. This mechanical outfit had to be push-started by the driver, and once the engine was running, the driver would have to spring smartly on to the moving contraption. This new mode of transport fascinated our new doctor, who could often be seen helping to repair similar machines that had broken down, as was their wont, in those pioneering days of transport. Knights of the road stick together – help one another in times of trouble was the motto! Alas, how times have changed.

We were also expected to give aid to our hard-pressed doctor when accidents happened. My father, who had passed his St John Ambulance tests, was often called upon to render assistance. I remember one very snowy day, with deep drifts everywhere, and a bitterly cold wind which whipped up small particles of snow into your face and eyes, making them smart painfully, coming across a young girl I knew, named Florence Grey. She had foolishly ventured out on her bicycle, and had plunged head first into a snow-drift. I went to her help, and on picking her up, suspected she had broken her collar bone. We made our way to the surgery as soon as we could and the doctor quickly diagnosed a dislocated shoulder, whereupon, looking at this strong young girl, he told me he would need help as he might have to use chloroform. After we had divested Florence of her thick outer garments and her blouse, the doctor attempted to replace the dislocated shoulder, but to no avail.

'I thought so,' he said, 'she's much too strong for me – you will have to do it.'

He helped poor Florence shed more underwear until she

was down to her vest (I have teased Florence about this at odd times over the years, telling her that I bet I was the first chap to see her in her vest, much to her amusement). The doctor then showed me how to feel for the hole in the shoulder muscle, torn when the joint was dislocated, and how to pop the bone back in place. I did this after two attempts, whilst the doctor administered the chloroform – poor Florence!

This type of country doctoring was not at all unusual. I shall never forget coming a cropper off my motor cycle at speed. What a mess I was in – my clothes were in shreds, my laced-up boots were ripped off and I was covered in blood from head to foot – not a pretty sight! My worst injury seemed to be to my knee and I reached home with great difficulty, frightening my mother in no uncertain manner. She sent a neighbour for the doctor, praying that he would come at once, which, in fact, he did. As I lay back in a fireside chair, he examined me quickly, concentrating on my kneecap which appeared to be broken in half. Remarking that, 'We must do something with that,' he attempted to sew it up, but unfortunately the needle would not go through my gristly knee, and one after the other they broke until, in desperation, he turned to my mother and asked if she had a bodkin or a packing needle. When mother produced several of this type of needle, he chose the biggest and attacked my knee again. Still having difficulty in getting the needle through, he picked up a fire-lighting stick from the hearth and proceeded to push the needle in and out with the aid of this piece of wood – all this with no anaesthetic. After swathing me in bandages, the doctor told my mother to get me upstairs to bed and to keep me there until he said I could get up.

After a week or more my leg began to smell dreadfully and the putrid stench which filled the room as it wafted up from the bed whenever I moved is difficult to describe. It made Mother feel quite sick. At last she could stand it no longer and sent for the doctor, whereupon he threw back the bedclothes and sniffed at my knee, remarking, 'That's just how I like it to smell. You'll see that I'm right.' And, indeed, he was.

After some weeks had elapsed he visited me again, and after cutting off the stiff matted bandages exposed a clean white knee, perfectly healed, apart from a ridge across my kneecap. When the stitches were removed, I was told I must use crutches for a week or two, gradually bending my knee when I felt like it. How's that for a bit of home doctoring?

I formed a close, respectful friendship with our old doctor and felt rather put out when he attended my wife at the birth of our son. He shouted for me to come up, and meeting me at the top of the stairs, clapped his hand on my shoulder, saying, 'You've got a son. I hope he's a better man than his father!' The penny did not drop until later that this was a kind wish, since if every new generation proves better than the old one, we will in time get some super young ones.

He must have had this in mind when I sent a friend and workmate for a medical in order that he could drive a public service bus. I felt a little apprehensive about his vision as at that time he had rather a nervous blink.

'How did you get on, Harry?' I asked.

'I passed A.1,' was the reply.

'How did he test your eyes?' I wanted to know.

'He didn't,' was the reply, 'he told me he had brought me into the world, knew all the family history and assured me I was okay.' This proved to be so as Harry passed quite a few medicals in later years and is still alive to tell the tale.

Early in my adolescence I had what I can only describe as the happiest job of my working life, that of an auxiliary postman. My day started at 5.30 am when I had to take mail to the outlying farms and cottages. I walked and cycled miles in a day, up muddy farm tracks, over hills, through woods and across streams, an idyllic occupation for a healthy, country-loving youth. One of my perks was to collect medicine bottles from these off-the-beaten-track homes and take them to the doctor's for a refill, which I delivered the next day, for which I received twopence. One day, after travelling miles, I discovered that a cork had come out of a bottle in my post bag, staining quite a few letters in the process. I was relieved to find that a small quantity of the medicine remained in the bottle which I proceeded to fill up from a spring in a remote field called Hollowell, and after shaking the bottle up well to add a little colour, I delivered it to the occupier of a small cottage, tongue in cheek, praying she would not die because of my deception. I was very relieved to see this nice old lady a week later, waving an empty bottle for me to take a refill. She handed me my twopence and I was instructed to ask the doctor for a repeat of this new medicine. 'It has done me a power of good – I haven't felt so well for years,' said dear Miss Leeson.

I explained to Dr Hope what I had done, and he laughingly said, 'It's better if you take more water with it!'

referring, I'm sure, to his favourite tipple. However, Miss Leeson thrived for years on the watered down mixture. Knowing how our ancestors held some of these wells in high esteem – we have so many around us – could my bottle-filling well, known to me as Hollowell, have been Holywell, its magical waters giving a new lease of life to this dear old lady?

Talking of medicine bottles and their corks reminds me of the doctor's foreign-made car which burnt its clutch out the day before he was to take it on a continental holiday, touring France and Belgium. In desperation he came to me begging me to do something about it. I removed the gear box and clutch plates (in those days the clutch ran in oil), exposing the burnt-off cork plate. We telephoned far and wide for a replacement plate but all to no avail. Poor Dr Hope, he was so disappointed at the loss of, or at least the postponement of, a well-deserved holiday. I remarked that if I had dozens of corks, I was sure I could make a temporary repair, to which the doctor replied that if medicine bottle corks would do, he had hundreds of them. To cut a long story short, I worked well into the night cutting, filing and fitting those corks – and it worked – lasting the life of the car. How nice it is to look back with pride on the self-sufficiency of our village.

This village of ours had a very close relationship with Dr Barnardo's Homes, and over the years dozens of small boys and girls from these homes came to live here. The people with whom they lived were so glad of the extra money which helped considerably with the difficult task of making ends meet on the pitiful wages most of the menfolk brought home. But it was not just extra money they were concerned about, they were also anxious about the welfare of the children, and they took them to their hearts, loving and treating them as if they were their own.

The children stayed here from an early age until leaving school at the age of fourteen, then many of the boys went into the Navy or were found homes in our developing colonies. It is enlightening when turning the pages of our church's Visitors' Book, to read the names of children and grandchildren of our foster children of yester-year. Visitors came from many parts of the globe to see the village which welcomed their fathers and grandfathers so many years ago. Of course, quite a number have stayed here all their lives and are at one with us all.

My friend Frances often visits one or other of her twin foster brothers, flying to Australia to see Ted and journeying north to stay with Dick (I think I've got it right – they are so alike I never did know which was which), and the grown-up children of the Australian twin come over to stay with Frances for weeks at a time. So many of the grown foster children are, and have been, so supportive of their foster parents, which proves what a loving relationship they must have enjoyed.

Thinking about the colonies reminds me of a funny little happening of some years ago. I sat looking out of our living-room window one afternoon when I saw two men, one elderly, looking at our house and garden. They looked like Americans by their dress, and, thinking they might be lost, I went outside to ask them if I could be of any help. The elder of the two said, 'I was born in this house over seventy years ago,' to which I replied, 'You are not

Americans – you are Canadians, and your name is Propert.' I was asked how I knew this and I told them their name was on the deeds of the house, which mentioned a family of locksmiths who had lived here before the First World War and had emigrated to Canada.

I invited them to come in and they fetched their two wives from the car, then with great excitement, Mr Propert showed them over the house, taking them to the bedroom where he was born and assuring them that the house had not changed one bit over the years.

'Just look at the door locks,' he said, and told us how he and his brother would say, when they were at work making modern keys in Canada, 'Do you remember the keys back in the old home? You could kill a chicken with them!'

Mr Propert told me that the last time he had visited the village was with the Canadian forces during the First World War. After questioning me about any changes that had taken place over the years, he decided to look around some of his old haunts and well-remembered focal points. Mrs Propert, a very attractive, nicely dressed, slim woman, with not a hair out of place, asked if she could stay with us whilst the rest of her family explored the village, and, of course, we were very pleased to have her stay. The family had hardly left the house before Mrs Propert told us about her husband's boyhood sweetheart, his 'English Rose', he called her. She went on to say how, over the years, she had had her leg pulled unmercifully over this English beauty. After some hesitation she mentioned this girl's name, asking if we knew her, was she married, was she still alive? We both knew this elderly lady well. Unfortunately, over the years, she had become a recluse, very careless in her dress and bowed down with age, tending her animals on her smallholding, with a house full of cats for company. We understood that she, like so many women of her age, had lost her sweetheart in the First World War.

Whilst feeling very sorry for this rather odd old lady, I could not resist describing her to Mrs Propert, painting not too unkind a picture of her English rival. About a year after the Properts' returned home to Canada, we received an invitation to visit them for their Golden Wedding celebrations. Enclosed with the invitation was a letter from Mrs Propert telling us how she, her two daughters and eleven grandchildren often had a quiet laugh with one another about Grampy's 'English Rose', with her stockings tied up with binder twine – never letting on to the old man when he teased them, that they knew his rose had grown a little thorny and not quite so sweet smelling as of yester-year.

I am so glad Mr Propert came to see his old home before passing away about two years after his visit. Perhaps, one day, some of his grandchildren will come to see the house he was born in. Alas, his 'English Rose' has also passed away.

Chapter 16

Dick and Denis: Two Old Men Recalling Their Youth – Denis Judd, Postman, Garage and Bus Proprietor – Dick Haynes, Farm Worker, Dustman, Poet and Respected Lay Preacher, Skilled in All Country Crafts

I have already mentioned how I enjoyed delivering the mail to the lone farms and isolated cottages in our district. There was, however, one farm I was loath to go to known as Charlwelton Hill Farm. The farm was kept by a very aggressive farmer who had a chip on his shoulder; he seemed to derive pleasure from upsetting all those with whom he came in contact. This was a great pity, because the farmhouse stood so well, with wonderful views for miles over the surrounding countryside. If you walked a short distance along the ridge of the hill on which the house stood, to the site of an ancient windmill, you could, on a clear day, see the Cotswolds and the Malvern Hills. I am told that on an exceptionally clear day, with the aid of a telescope, the mountains of Wales could be seen. Be that as it may, I would often think, why be so grumpy in such marvellous surroundings?

The farmhouse was approached by crossing three fields, the first field being comparatively easy. The second field began to rise steeply, making walking quite hard work, but the third and last field was very steep indeed, ending up with a sharp incline which left you so breathless that it was a relief to reach the house with the mail. So often the letter would be one with a halfpenny stamp affixed and unsealed. Everyone knew these were either advertising material or, more often than not, unwanted bills. Most people living in not easily accessible places would tell me to keep back the letters with a halfpenny stamp until I had a first-class letter to deliver (1 d stamp and sealed).

One day I was delivering a halfpenny letter to the bad-tempered farmer on the hill, when he remarked, 'Is this all you have for me?'

'Yes, that's all,' was my reply, and thinking of other people in like situations, I said, 'Need I come all the way up here with just a bill?' I asked this with tongue in cheek, quite expecting to be refused, and I was totally unprepared for the change which came over the man at my request. He went beserk, shouting and screaming at me and threatening to give me a good hiding. He looked so fierce that I threw my mailbag to the ground and prepared to do battle. This positive attitude took the wind out of the sails of my aggressive opponent because he turned tail and retreated to the house, muttering blood-curdling threats.

The next morning I climbed steadily up towards the farmhouse, breathing a sigh of relief when I saw no sign of the truculent farmer. But when I was half-way up the third and last field a very fierce bull emerged from a barn and, on spotting me, began pawing the ground, snorting and tossing his head from side to side, digging his horns in the turf and showing obvious displeasure at the sight of the postman intruder. I made my way as quickly as possible, without actually running, towards the gate, and had just reached it when the old bull came down at a fast trot, bellowing with rage because I had evaded him. He really meant business. My word, I thought, like farmer, like bull! I had to make a detour over several fields in order to approach the farm from the rear, staying well clear of the bull which was still showing signs of being upset. This little saga was enacted for several consecutive mornings, with me not daring to enter the third and last field on account of the bull being deliberately let out as I approached. As I was not at all pleased at having to make a detour each day, I left a note at the house saying that if the bull was not kept shut up until after my visit I would not deliver any more mail.

The next morning I was relieved to see that the bull had been kept in, and I began to make my way by the direct route when out rushed the animal in a terrible rage, charging down the hill at full gallop. With the bull on my heels, I climbed on top of the hedge, grasping a low branch of a tree and swinging myself out of his way. He burst through the hedge as if it were non-existent, continuing into the next field, where, to his pleasure and my relief, he spied a bunch of young heifers. All war-like thoughts left him as he turned on the charm with these innocent young ladies. There is a sequel to this tale as, because I refused to deliver his mail, the farmer lost his existing milk contract whereby the milk was picked up at the farm gate on the road, and so was forced to take his milk to the railway station in order to catch the early train to London, picking up his mail at the post office on his return journey. What a relief!

After a week or so, my farmer, true to form, fell foul of the station staff who, one day, could not stand his bullying any longer and thrust him into the guard's van, locking the door behind him and giving the right away signal to the engine driver. The cursing farmer was taken six miles up the line to the next station, and this meant a long walk back for the old misery. When would he learn?

It was to be expected that these lone farms were guarded by sheep dogs, and some of these were of a semi-wild nature. When I approached the buildings they would make off up the field, only to wait in hiding in order to attack me, quite unexpectedly, on my return journey, or slink up behind me, crouching on their tummies and nipping me on the back of my calf, bruising my leg, even through my wellingtons. This mode of attack seems to be a speciality with some sheep dogs. My only defence against this type of attack was to make friends with them, and make friends I did. One dog would come at least half a mile to meet me each morning, racing me back to the farm where he lived. Unfortunately, he would wait for me on a Sunday (my day off), and not being accustomed to roads, was run over and killed – what a shame.

If ever I lived on a lone farm I would choose a flock of geese for guardians. Whenever I have encountered them on a farm they would surround me, making enough noise to waken the dead, hissing and pecking my legs into the bargain. The best way to deal with geese is on the table at Michaelmas!

When talking one day to my old friend and ex-workmate, Dick Haynes, as old men do, we began to reminisce about our youth. I recalled the early days when I was a postman, remarking on how many rivers began their life in about a six-mile radius of our village, and also, how many farms there were with names ending in well. I mentioned Charwell (or Char'ell as it is known locally), where the river Cherwell rises in a farmhouse cellar. It can be heard gushing out, forming a pool by the house, and after filling the pool to the brim it goes on its journey towards the village of Charwelton (Cherwell town). The infant Cherwell passes under an ancient pack-horse bridge at Charwelton, getting stronger by the mile as it makes its way to Oxford where, for some reason unknown to me, it changes its name to Isis before joining the Thames and meandering on to the sea. Dick remarked, 'I worked around Char'ell.' I then mentioned another well – Pitwell – saying I felt sure this was an abbreviation of St Peter's Well, and Dick said, 'I worked there, too.' 'Dick,' I said, 'why don't you tell me how you started work?'

So Dick began: 'My life was the life of the average village boy – I left school at the age of fourteen at Easter 1923. I had no work until July. My first job was on a farm called Pitwell, which is, as you know, about a mile from the village. There seemed to be three bosses and two workmen and myself. I soon found out that I was the whipping boy, for if on any occasion we were a few minutes late getting to work, which was very rare – we always walked together – it was always me that got the telling off in front of the others, and so it was for most things that went wrong on the farm. But I have never regretted that first job, for it was a great experience to find out what hard work was all about and to learn the various skills that an all-round farm labourer needs if he is going to work with horses and cattle of all kinds, to be able to milk, to plough, and to understand all the operations that are used in arable farming.

'When I reached the age of sixteen I was asked to find another job because it meant having an insurance card and putting on a 9d stamp, and the boss did not want to pay this. I found another job in the village helping with the milking night and morning and taking care of young stock. New milking regulations came into force and the milking shed was closed, both we milkmen losing our jobs. I was now about nineteen years old.

'After a time I found a job as shed boy on Charwelton Parkgate Ironstone. I had a varied job to do, getting oil out of the stores for the engines and steam navvies, looking after the engine that pumped water from the pond at Cherwell Farm (where the river Cherwell rises in the farm cellar) to the mines at Bromtree. I was, in fact, a "go-for" boy – going for this and going for that! I did learn quite a bit as a mate to the blacksmith, carpenter and fitter when they came from other pits. Alas, then the great slump came, which meant I was without a regular job for about three years.

'There were times when I was able to find a day's work threshing. I remember one occasion when threshing – we got to the bottom of the rick and we discovered it was rat infested; they had burrowed down in the straw base of the rick, and that day I brought out with my bare hands seventy-three live rats, two or three at a time. I threw them at the wall and the other chaps finished them off – all this with no bites to my hands. I remember getting bitten badly when catching about twenty mice in the bottom of a corn bin on one farm I worked at.

'I did have one good summer helping with hay and harvest; in fact it went on well into the autumn doing about 120 chains of ditching and draining. I had lots of fun on the farms at this time – I must tell you some time.

'In 1934 I was offered a regular job on a farm in the village. I learned thatching and how to drive a tractor and motor car. There was no refuse collector in our village and the district council asked for tenders. The farmer I worked for put in a tender of £26 for a year's fortnightly collection. He got the contract and lucky old me, I became the first village dustman. There was so little room on an ordinary two-wheeled farm cart, even with high sides, and I sometimes got very angry about all the weeds and paper that were put in the bins, so one day, finding a piece of chalk, I wrote on the cart:

Burn your blinking weeds and paper,
Do you think I do this for a caper?
Don't you think it's a dirty trick
Trying to bust old dustman Dick?

'Mr Adams the grocer gave me a packet of Woodbines for this rhyme. Another verse I put on the cart when folk had killed a lot of poultry and had put the feathers loose in the bin so that they blew everywhere was:

It tries my patience right to the end,
Yes, right to the end of its tether,
That when you kill that old fat hen
You give *me* its blinking feathers.

'Another one I wrote:

> It makes me unhappy and all forlorn
> When you give me the clippings from your lawn.
> These are classed as weeds you know,
> If you can't burn them, let them grow.

'I used to make a special journey to fetch the ashes from Mr Wilmot's nursery. One day there was a lot of stones and bricks amongst the ashes. I complained, and Mr Wilmot said he would give me sixpence for a rhyme telling him off, so I wrote:

> I'll take your ashes and old tin cans
> And also your broken crockery,
> But with your old brick ends and stones
> You must try and make a rockery.

'I think people looked to see what would appear next. It may have amused some, but it did very little good. I think the final verse was:

> All good people that do dwell
> In this village we love so well,
> Please read this and inwardly learn
> That weeds and paper you must burn.'

Dick went on – 'In October 1937 I changed my job again to timber hauling.' 'Steady on Dick,' I said, 'it's time we were going home – you must tell me more another day.'

Chapter 17

A Christmas Fairyland and How Officialdom Can Change the Face of a Village Yet Benefit the Health of its People

Northamptonshire is situated in the very centre of England, always rather an independent county, its people feeling they neither belonged to East Anglia or Mercia. The buildings were different in style to either of those ancient territories, and because of the belt of oolite limestone sweeping up from the Cotswolds, passing through the length of the county and disappearing into Lincolnshire, they were constructed with this ready-to-hand building material. This stone, when thatched with straw or slated with the well known Collyweston stone slates mined in the north of the county, and because of the very steep pitched roofs, gave a style which compared very favourably with that well-known beauty spot, the Cotswolds. But we are comparatively undiscovered, and therefore enjoy a more undisturbed rural life, particularly at weekends and during the holiday season. I am not sure if this is an advantage or a disadvantage, as prosperity seems to come in the wake of tourists and the villages might benefit from an influx of visitors.

Naturally, being so far from the coast, we miss the warmth of the sea, and because of the open surroundings, together with the extra few feet of altitude, get rather more than our fair share of snow. How I have enjoyed and battled with this over the years. At one time during my posting years I harnessed a police dog we had named Peter to a sledge and took the mail to villages, which were cut off for some days. My mother packed up a haversack of food for me and the dog, and off we would go. What fun it was to walk over snow-buried hedges and gates, making a more or less direct route to the various villages and calling at outlying farms if they were not too far out of my way.

As a rule, after it has snowed for days on end, the sun comes out and shines from a cloudless azure sky. This colour blue can only be seen and appreciated when standing on dazzling white snow, and what with the clean cut air, the warmth of the sun on my face and that heavenly blue sky reaching as far as my eyes could see, how I enjoyed those overland journeys. It was easy to imagine I was in Canada or Austria as I trudged along with my faithful companion pulling the sledge. No thought entered my head of how much I was earning or when I would get back home – just a wonderful feeling of well-being. It was so different in later years when we were cut off by the snow and I had to think about the fifteen or more buses I ran; the coal business I owned which supplied many villages in the district; my repair garage and petrol pumps – all at a complete standstill. How would I be able to meet my outgoings and pay the men etc? Quite a headache, particularly one year, 1947, when we were immobile for four weeks. No sooner was a road dug out than it was filled in by wind-driven snow during the night. And so it went on, day after day – my buses were unable to work for the whole of that month.

I remember one Christmas when my mother's younger sister Freda, together with her husband George and small daughter Jean, came to spend the holiday with us (this was before I was married). No sooner had they arrived than it began to snow and continued to snow all Christmas Eve and all through Christmas Day without ceasing. When we awoke on Boxing Day morning, the sun shone on a clean new world and a fairy-tale landscape could be seen from our cottage windows. Freda, who was a cheerful, happy young woman, always ready with a song sung in a nice contralto voice, wanted to venture out and explore the changed new world straight away. My mother, who was so much older than Freda, persuaded her to wait until after lunch, saying, 'George will be unable to walk in the snow – Jean will want to go with you and its much too deep for her,' etc., etc. (George had lost a leg in the war.) However, as soon as Boxing Day lunch was over and we had washed up, Freda said, 'Come along, Denis, let's go out now, I can't wait much longer.' So Freda and I explored the village, stopping many times to admire the real old-fashioned Christmas card setting.

We had arranged to meet George and my father, so we made our way slowly towards the Priors Marston road, a high, wind-swept road bordering on Warwickshire, which I knew would be utterly and completely blocked and hidden and, sure enough, the scene I hoped to show Freda was there in all its glory. The wind had whipped up huge drifts of pristine whiteness, unblemished by humans or wildlife, and resembling fluffy icing sugar – I had never seen it looking more beautiful. Freda, who was thrilled by this white fairyland, asked me to lift her up and stand her on this winter tableland. I understood how she felt and looking at her husband George, who had so manfully struggled along with the help of my father, I asked, 'What am I to do?'

'Put her on,' said George.

I kicked some steps up the side of a drift then reached down, picking up Freda who was as light as a feather, and deposited her feet first on the top-most drift.

Freda immediately sank to her waist in the snow, and as she struggled, shrieking with happy, almost hysterical laughter, so she sank deeper. In the end I had to rescue her from becoming entombed. When her feet were on firmer ground we discovered her boots were full, her stockings plastered and her knickers snow encrusted to above the waist. Her hat was a little to one side and she clung to me as we all collapsed with laughter, the happiest laughter coming from the breathless Freda.

'I have always wanted to do that,' she cried.

We quickly made our way homewards, whereupon my worried mother made Freda change her wet clothes and sit by a roaring fire, sipping a hot drink. That Boxing Day evening, mother, Freda and I had quite a few warming drinks.

We were all of a glow when George, who had been out with my father, came in. He, too, had been celebrating in no uncertain manner, declaring repeatedly in a loud voice, 'I have not enjoyed myself so much for fifty years!' (At the time he was twenty-nine!!)

Quite a few years after this happy Christmas I was once again lifting Freda in very heart-breaking circumstances.

Freda, poor girl, was very seriously afflicted with rheumatoid arthritis which became progressively worse in a comparatively short period of time. This dreadfully painful disease did not stop at a few joints, a knee or a hip perhaps, but took over her whole body – however, she bore it bravely. All kinds of treatment were tried but to no avail, and in desperation she went for treatment to the Spa in Bath. We knew the waters there were supposed to help, as indeed I think they do, if only to support the body at the right density at a comforting temperature, enabling seized joints to be moved and massaged in order to try and get them working again. But I'm afraid the sufferer stood little chance of being cured.

We took Freda to Bath in a big old Daimler I owned, visiting her often during her stay whenever George could get time off from the office. She was so pleased to see us all and we were able to wheel her through the beautiful gardens and take her for a drive in the car when she felt well enough. Thank goodness those old cars had a wide and strong running-board to step on to when entering or getting out of the roomy back seat, as without this I could not have managed to lift Freda out of her wheelchair and into the car. How her poor bones creaked and complained as I lifted this frail young Aunt from one to the other. I think this was about the first time in my life I felt compassion, and I prayed that she would not break in my arms. My wife, who helped me, remembers it all too well and was so considerate to my mother when she was struck down with arthritis in later years. When we grumble about the 'screws' and have joints that complain at times, we look at one another and say, 'Poor old Gran, poor Freda, how they must have suffered.' Needless to say, Freda's frail, pain-racked body could not cope, and she passed away when Jean was about ten years old.

I did not see as much of Jean as I would have liked for some years, although she kept in constant touch with my mother. Then came the Second World War, making visiting difficult. One day I had to kill some time in Banbury and was watching a convoy of army trucks and half-track vehicles being very skilfully parked. All of these vehicles were driven by ATS girls and I marvelled at the dexterity these young girls had acquired. Half-track vehicles were not the easiest things to manoeuvre. However, the whole operation was completed in no time at all, and the drivers began to jump out of the cabs to stretch their legs. They all looked so fit and well and I thought to myself, 'Girls, you are doing a grand job for the war effort.' To my surprise, I heard my name called out by one of these young ladies – 'Denis, how lovely to see you!' I stared at this smartly uniformed, self-possessed ATS girl as she strode towards me, white teeth flashing in a broad smile – 'Uncle-cousin Denis!!' she said. Could this possibly be the baby with wet nappies I had nursed so many times in the past when her mother had dumped her into my bed in the early mornings so that she could snatch a few extra minutes rest from her robust offspring? Sure enough it was Jean. I was thrilled to see her after a space of several war years, and we gave one another a hug and kiss, whereupon the ATS sergeant in charge said in a loud voice, 'What's all this?'

'Not to worry, Sarg,' said Jean, 'he is my cousin but I call him uncle.'

'I've heard those tales before,' said the protective sergeant, 'I don't want to lose sight of you – we move off in twenty minutes.'

We had such a lot to talk about in those twenty minutes. I'm so glad we met as I was able to tell my mother and father about Jean's exploits, making them feel very proud of their niece.

Jean married a nice young chap called Bob and they live happily together in a village about twelve miles from us, just a short distance from where our grandfather met and courted his teacher. Jean, who was one of our young bridesmaids fifty years ago, has, I am pleased to say, kept in touch over the years.

There lived at one time in a village quite close to where Jean and Bob live, a zealous and, in my opinion, occasionally misguided, council official who, because of his searching and prying into sanitary conditions in village and farm alike, earned the name of Nuisance Inspector from the local people. Whenever neighbours fell out over a bonfire or the disposal of garden rubbish, the one cry was, 'I'll tell the Nuisance Inspector about you.' Very few people were completely free from the threat of this official as whenever you did any alterations or made what you thought were improvements to your property, you felt a little scared in case he found out and would not agree. I know the correct procedure was to ask permission first, but this was not the way of the village folk who were an independent lot and hated any interference with their plans.

Deep down we knew he was right over so many things, and when it came to sorting out our antiquated drains, and seeing that an uncontaminated water supply was easily available to one and all, we began to see the light, and no longer said, 'What was good enough for my old Dad was good enough for me.' We remembered those who had died young, and we also remembered the yellow-coloured van that could often be seen taking poor sick children to the local Isolation Hospital at Staverton when epidemics were rife.

It was also a great relief to be able to have your bedroom windows open on warm moonlit nights, especially on the nights that in the recent past had been reserved for the annual emptying of those dreadful old privy pits, which were much in use in remote villages.

In my early days, as had been the custom for years, the privy was always built right at the bottom of the garden, as far away from the house as possible, for obvious reasons. They were roughly constructed with elm boards, built over a deep pit with a wooden top which usually had two large holes cut out of it for Mum and Dad and a smaller one for the children – we used to call them three-seaters – not very comfortable when the cold winds blew. You certainly wasted no time in your old privy. These seats were posed over the noisome, deeply dug pit which was constructed with a trapdoor to the rear to facilitate the yearly emptying. What a job for some poor, and in most cases, elderly man, no doubt driven by poverty to earn the fifteen shillings for his night's work. I might add he collected his money on the following day when he was presentable.

The conveyance used for this fearsome task was known as the midnight chariot, and in the course of general conversation you might be asked whether you heard the midnight chariot last night, to which your reply would often be, 'No, but I smelt it!' If you were returning home from a dance or a party you fled at top speed when you heard the sound of the iron wheels of this grim, dimly lit, foul-smelling monster. Looking back, it is hard to believe that such conditions existed in our youth.

I can remember one Leekie French, a likeable old character who ran a weekly service with a hand-cart which he used for emptying the lavatory buckets from some of the more newly built cottages. He would trundle this specially designed, galvanized iron-wheeled contraption along with complete nonchalance, pipe in mouth, a smoky old oil lamp swinging from the handle dimly lighting his way. One dark night his routine was disturbed by some of his own children; two of his older daughters lay in wait in the churchyard for this custodian of other peoples' waste, springing out on him with blood-curdling shrieks, dressed as ghosts, causing their father to let go of the handle of the hand-cart, spilling the contents over the 'ghosts' and himself. I am told these 'ghosts' had a very warm welcome when they arrived home smelling of 'sweet violets'!

When examining the deeds of our house, dating back to the year 1753, I noticed with a smile that in beautiful copper-plate writing on a well-drawn plan, almost taking pride of place, the word 'Privy' was written. This was at the very edge of the plan, indicating that it was situated as far from the house and out-buildings as possible. No wonder the centuries old holly tree which now lives on that spot grows with such strength and vigour, producing in abundance masses of luscious red berries in time for Christmas (and the birds) year after year.

When describing the wooden trapdoor to the rear of the privy pit, I am reminded of a mischievous relation of mine who lived at a lone farm a couple of miles away. He would often come down to the village to play Fox and Hounds with the village boys, and on one never-to-be-forgotten occasion fell head over heels through one of these trapdoors, which no doubt was rotten with age. Fortunately he was rescued by Mrs Titchy Smith, a kindly village shopkeeper, who stripped him and scrubbed him clean before dressing him in some of her children's clothes and sending him on his journey home, sadder but no doubt wiser.

How glad we all were to see the end of these antiquated contraptions – well done, Mr Nuisance Inspector! We had to take our hats off to him when, with grim determination, he ensured that the ministry regulations were fully implemented on the milking farms. This must have been a difficult task as it was often found that the milk being produced was contaminated through the unhygienic conditions that prevailed in some of the cowsheds. It was also discovered that in some cases sixty per cent of the cows had TB or reacted positively to TB tests. No wonder tuberculosis was not unknown among the people. It must have been very difficult to have to break the news to a farmer that his prized cow, the best of the herd in his opinion, was a reactor and must be destroyed. No wonder the Inspector was disliked and feared whenever he put in an appearance, but I, and many others, think he did a good job.

Where I felt he made a mistake was in his often spoken threat of getting every thatched cottage in the village condemned and pulled down. This, I felt, was destroying the rural atmosphere that had been enjoyed by villagers over the centuries. Council officialdom seemed hell-bent on getting the people out of their cottages and into the council houses on a new estate that had been built for just this purpose. The old cottagers did not take kindly to this move as they were perfectly happy in their picturesque surroundings, with rents at 1/6d (7½p) to 2/6d 12½p) per week. Who could blame them? They did not want the upheaval of moving.

In answer to this refusal to comply, the Nuisance Inspector's next move was to get the thatched cottages condemned by putting pressure on the landlords, using thinly disguised threats about the power of office he held, and what was required of landlords by the new acts now in force, and this, in most cases, did the trick. Many of these lovely old cottages were extremely old but not worn out. What a pity we did not have a committee for the preservation of rural England to turn to for help in those days. One man, just a little older than me, told me he could remember at least thirty thatched cottages in Westhorpe Lane alone – now there is one and people stop to photograph and sketch this remaining cottage to this day. How much better it would have been if the full complement of thirty cottages, together with the old Blackbird pub and the communal Westhorpe well had been left in this quiet, grassy banked, pleasant setting.

The slogan 'Health before Beauty' was the watchword of the day. I am not so sure that it applies nowadays, for the few remaining picturesque cottages are being keenly sought after and are changing hands at tens of thousands of pounds.

A case in point is that out of the seven nice stone cottages that I once owned, three with tiled roofs and four of them thatched, which I reluctantly sold because of talk of compulsory purchase, etc., one changed hands two years ago for £115,000; so different from the £650 I gave for the seven and the £1,300 I sold the complete seven for. If both myself and the Nuisance Inspector could have seen into the future, I would not have sold and he would not have been so eager to condemn.

Chapter 18

A Phone Call Out of the Blue and Some Lovely Old Country Characters

When I look back on my life and try to make comparisons money-wise with wages and the cost of living from when we were first married in 1937 and the present day lifestyle, I feel sure there is very little to choose between the years. My wife may have started keeping house on 30/– (£1.50) a week, and out of that paid my mother 5/– (25p) rent for our cottage, but we managed very well; I had about 10/– a week to run a car on, which paid for trips to Banbury to the cinema, a drink and a fish and chip supper afterwards, all for 5/– for the two of us. An enjoyable night out and money still in our pockets – not bad!

We completely furnished our small cottage for £77, all paid for at one go out of the savings accumulated during our courting years. If we could pay into the Post Office Savings Bank 7/6d (37½p) weekly between us to add to our other small savings, we were in clover.

I have bought many a bull-nosed Morris or Austin 7 HP for £2.50 to £3.00, have run it for several months, and after cleaning it and doing odd jobs to it, have sold it for a small profit. Very cheap family motoring.

In retrospect I feel that the two to three years before the Second World War must have been the years during which you received the best value for money and for your labour. Most articles you bought lasted for years. We still have so many things that we started out with well over fifty years ago.

I sometimes smile to myself when I remember my wife asking Mr Montgomery, the butcher, to please bring a smaller joint of beef for the weekend as we had such a job to eat it all up in time for next weekend. She also told him we were fed up with beef every day in some form or another and would like a change in the week. This massive joint of best beef would cost us 4/6 (22½p). I should like a 4/6d joint to last a whole week nowadays!

When I write about the years just before the Second World War, I am reminded of the terrible hardship endured up until then if you were out of work and your dole money ran out. What a degrading position to be in, for no matter how you struggled against selling nearly all of your prized possessions, it was a losing battle. No matter how you tried for work the answer was invariably, 'Sorry – we have no vacancies – I don't know how I keep those on that I've already got.'

This state of affairs was brought home to me one evening as I was locking up my garage workshop when the telephone rang. On answering it a voice said, 'This is Shell Mex from Leicester, is that Mr Judd?' (Mine was a Shell garage.)

'Yes,' I replied, 'can I help you?'

The voice from Shell Mex went on, 'Do you know a man called Harry Jones in your village, one of our old pipe and pump fitters?'

'Yes, I do,' I answered, 'I know Harry Jones, but I didn't

know he was one of your pump fitters – he hasn't worked for years.'

The voice continued, 'Mr Judd, would you be kind enough to tell him that if he is at our Leicester depot by 8.00 tomorrow morning he can have his old job back.'

'Right,' I said, 'I will pop up to his house right away and tell him the good news.' 'Now,' said the Shell representative, 'he must be there on time, otherwise the job will be given to another fitter.'

I immediately made my way to Harry Jones's house. He had married a local girl and he, his wife and two children lived in a council house.

As I knocked at the door I could hear someone singing an old nursery rhyme in a quiet Welsh voice. I gently opened the door and found Harry sitting in front of a wet wood fire, cuddling his small son on his knee.

'Harry,' I said, 'if you can be at Leicester by 8.00 tomorrow morning your old job will be waiting for you.' He burst into tears, and stared at me with a look of disbelief on his thin face.

'You wouldn't play a cruel joke on me, would you Denis?' he asked.

'No, it's genuine enough, Harry,' I assured him.

'I'll be there, I'll be there,' he kept repeating, 'I'll have to start walking as soon as Ida comes home.' (Leicester was forty-five miles away.) His wife Ida was out plucking and dressing some poultry for Christmas for a local farmer for 1/6d (7½p) a bird, which was untold wealth for her just before Christmas.

Harry started pacing about, asking me whether I thought he could do the journey in time. He also said what a pity it was he had had to sell his bike in order to buy food. I promised him that I had a bike he could borrow for a week or two until he was able to afford one, or better still, I would sell it to him for 10/– (50p). I cheered him up further by telling him he could pay me back a little at a time when he was able to.

When I saw Harry a year or two later, looking so well and happy with his wife and children in the family car, enjoying a holiday visit to our village, I could not help but think of the night I took the good news to him. For years I have had a picture in my mind of that dim, cold, candle-lit room, with a father trying to bring comfort to his son by cuddling him for warmth and singing to him in soft Welsh tones – how cruel unemployment was when your dole money ran out.

The real old countryman did not fare so badly as he had his country craft and the know-how to help him fill his cooking pot one way or another. These crafts were handed down through the ages and the art of escaping detection and severe retribution from the landowners and magistrates, whose punishments were very harsh in the olden days, was instilled into the later generations when punishment was more in keeping with the times.

Possibly, if caught at the glorious sport of poaching, if the quarry had been rabbits and not game, a 10/– fine was usually the case, but how much more exciting it was *not* to be caught, especially if you had, through your skill and stealth, purloined one of his Lordship's hares or pheasants. When these escapades were recounted by the true country cottagers there was much amusement among the listeners. I have, at times, been taken to see their ferrets which were kept in cages in their gardens and sheds, all so painstakingly tended. The ferrets would be lovingly spoken to when taken out of their cages, their good qualities pointed out and their skills discussed with fervour. The line ferret was shown with pride – a length of thin cord was attached to a collar, enabling the poacher to control the fearsome little beast. Some could, however, be trusted to hunt on their own, and would soon bolt a rabbit or two into the nets which were placed over the rabbits' bolt hole, the ferret then returning to its master when called.

I have been asked many times to put my hands into a cage and lift a ferret out, but when I looked into those pale pink baleful eyes, and noticed the sharp little teeth with which these fierce little animals were armed, I chickened out. Discretion, I felt, was the better part of valour.

This was not so with your true ferret man who handled his pets with complete confidence. I think the ferrets knew this and would seldom bite their owners. However, I do remember one owner named Martin Treadwell who would, as was the custom when standing under the Cross Tree, have his ferret inside his shirt. You could see the bulges as the ferret moved around inside his shirt, travelling from front to back and up and down. At times out would pop a little head and Martin would comment, 'Look at the little beauty,' and then, when the head appeared out of his shirt neck band, he would say, as ferret looked at master, and master gazed at ferret, 'Give me a kiss then,' and ferret and master would rub noses. One day, however, the little beauty fastened his teeth in Martin's lower lip, hanging on like grim death (ferrets, once they bite will not let go – it's not in their nature). Martin shouted as loudly as his natural disability of having a short tongue and the added handicap of a ferret clinging to his lip, would allow, 'Frottle the little budder off!' With great difficulty he was freed from this passionate kiss. We all laughed and said it was a good job the leather belt holding up his trousers was tight around his waist and ferret proof, or we might have had difficulty in catching up with Martin!

Old Billy Lane was another character who brought his pet ferrets out in the evening, tucked inside his shirt. Billy was a timber carriage driver, and the control he had over the three, four or sometimes five horses (depending on the size of the tree he had loaded on the timber carriage), harnessed one in front of the other, had to be seen to be believed. This long train of horses and carriage could often be seen travelling our country roads, controlled by word of mouth only. Billy who sometimes could be seen sitting on the base of the shaft, or at other times walking, would direct his team either left or right with a, 'Gee back, whoa back,' or whatever command was necessary. On many occasions he would have to run to the rear of the carriage and wind large brake handles on tightly in order to stop the heavy load over-running the shaft horse, all this being done whilst the other horses plodded steadily on. We would often watch for him returning home with his long load to the timber yard. The tired horses would speed up when they realised they were nearly home, making the carriage swerve and sway, but Billy, with his 'Gee backs' and 'Whoa backs' would reach the end of his journey with a flourish. I never heard of him knocking down a gate-post during all his difficult manoeuvres, but I expect he must have done so at odd times.

One day I was talking to Mrs Lane, Billy's wife, and I remarked, 'You know, I think your Bill's a marvel – the miles he walks every day in charge of that unwieldy timber wagon and those huge horses – not many men could do it.'

'I know,' said little Mrs Lane, 'he does work hard, but you know he can be a bit awkward at times. When he was a young man he was very smart and well turned-out. He pestered me to get married, promising me the earth. He kept saying he would buy me a carriage and pair of high-steppers if only I would say "Yes".'

'Did you get your carriage and pair, Mrs Lane?' I asked.

'Not quite,' she replied. 'After we had been married some time I had a carriage, which was a pram, and a pair of lovely twin boys to ride in it! That was Billy Lane's carriage and pair, but I love them all.'

When I think about gateposts and Billy Lane, I am reminded of one year when I went haymaking on Manor Farm. My first job was to walk with a loaded four-wheeled wagon pulled by two large cart-horses to and from the hay field to the rick-yard in the manor grounds. The farmer issued all kinds of dire threats to me about what would happen if I knocked a gatepost out of the ground on my trips. Now, as the gateway was on a steep slope, the wagon huge and overloaded with loose hay, the poor shaft horse had great difficulty in holding the unwieldy load back. Consequently, we came out of the field at the run and how I missed the dreaded gateposts I shall never know, but miss them I did.

After a couple of days at this, the farmer decided that as I was a big strong boy I could go and start pitching hay and he would take over the driving to and fro. When we were having a meal break later on, the cowman came to the field ready to help us. How we all laughed when he told us that the Old Man (the farmer) had knocked a couple of posts down!

I lined up with the men when the first Saturday afternoon pay-day came round. We had to go to the kitchen window of the farmhouse for our money. Naturally, I, being the youngest, was last in the queue, waiting with great anticipation for the 14/– I had earned. When at last I approached the window the housewife asked me what I wanted and I answered, 'My wages, please.' I was told, 'We only pay those that work here regularly – you will have to wait until we have finished for yours.' I did feel disappointed, but there you are – if that was the rule, so be it.

I worked very hard for that farmer all through the season, going early in the mornings to turn the swathes by hand as, because of the very heavy crop, the swathe-turner would not do the job it was designed for. When the sun rose and dried out the dew, I would then pitch hay until dusk, going home tired and dirty, consoling myself by thinking of the lovely lot of money I would have at the end of it all. But, to my dismay, I never was paid for my slogging labour. Excuses were made, such as, 'You will have to wait until I go to the bank,' or, when challenged again, the reply would be, 'I will give it to your father,' etc. etc. But neither Father or I were paid for that season's work – it taught me a never-to-be-forgotten lesson.

When I started up in business I upped my charges to this particular farmer for the repairs I did to his machinery and for material supplied, with not one little prick of my conscience. As the kingfisher said one day to his mate, everything comes to the fellow who waits.

You can see how touchy farmers could be over their gates and gateposts, and they were just about the same, if not worse, when it came to damaging their hedges, unless it was the Hunt that caused the damage. If the Hunt was responsible they sent out posts and rails with a Hunt servant and paid for them to be erected, more often than not stopping up more gaps than they had created.

With damage to hedges in mind, I remember an old character we had in our neighbourhood known to us all as Titanic Tom. Tom could be seen every morning coming into the village with his tea-can and long ash walking stick, stepping out briskly and making his regular house-calls where he would politely ask for some hot water for his tea-can and, if possible, a pinch of tea and a spoonful of sugar. When these needs were satisfied he would move on to another house and beg for bread and a small piece of cheese. If the housewife could spare them, and I have never seen Tom refused these basics of life, he would often be given a great deal more.

The whole village liked this quietly spoken, gentle man. He had his routine, never taking advantage of the kindness people bestowed upon him, and all the children talked to him completely unafraid and at ease with him. I asked him one day why he was known as Titanic Tom. He replied that he was a survivor from the sinking of the *Titanic*, that enormous, supposedly unsinkable, passenger liner which struck an iceberg on its maiden voyage and foundered with such a terrible loss of life. As I listened to his Birmingham accent as he told me about the *Titanic*, I had difficulty in either believing or disbelieving him. I saw no reason why he should tell this unlikely story if it was not true, so he was given the benefit of the doubt.

I wondered if this dreadful catastrophe had deranged Tom's mind and whether that was the reason for his living the life of a hermit. Tom approached the village each morning from the direction of a very remote, hilly area known as Blackdown, quite off the beaten track. I made up my mind to try and discover Tom's hide-out so one day, together with a friend named Algy Young, whose father had at one time farmed Blackdown, we set off, anticipating the fire that Tom had to have in order to keep warm. I told Algy we would easily find his whereabouts because of the state of the hedges he had pulled, but this was not so as all the hedges were tall and overgrown, showing no sign of vandalism. During our search we espied a small, tumble-down barn. Very little was left of its original shape, but there, standing in its doorway under some tall bushes, was Tom. We were asked into his retreat and there, amongst lashings of hay and straw, with bundles of old overcoats, pots and tin cans galore, we discovered how Tom had lived for years.

In the smoke-filled atmosphere we talked for a long time, he so polite and, I am sure, enjoying our company, but we in turn found out no more about Tom – his past was a closed book. I did hear that a well-known village farmer, namely W.H. Potter, received a small monthly remittance from someone or other, which he carefully doled out to Tom each day – enough to buy his tobacco, no doubt! I am not sure what happened to Tom eventually, but his passing left quite a gap in the community.

Chapter 19

The Rich Pattern of Village Life Remembered

When I think about the country tradesmen who made up the rich patten of village life and try to remember all the tales I have been told about them by the old men of the village, I am daunted by the task of describing them all, so will just briefly mention a few from the outstanding number of tradesmen our village had.

There were forty-seven tradesmen and professional men in all, ranging from Rector and MD and Surgeon, Keeper of a Ladies Seminary, Shoemaker, Harnessmaker, Blacksmith, Ropemaker, Miller, Carpenter, Wheelwright, Stonemason, Millwright, Butcher, Baker, Keepers of Beer Houses, Schoolmaster, Inn-keepers and Maltsters, Watchmaker, Plumber, Glazier, Cooper, Castrator, Grocers, Chairmaker, Draper, Milliner, Carrier and Chimney-sweep. And so I could go on. I will just mention a few who had a bearing on my youth.

I remember the three roadmen we had who kept our village tidy. Charlie Gardner was one – he was such a chatterbox and would follow you for miles in order to keep you talking. He bragged that he was the only man in Byfield with two birthdays. Apparently the registrar came infrequently to the village, and by the time he called

Charlie's parents were not too sure whether he was born on the 10th or the 14th, so they settled for the 14th when, in fact, it was the 10th. Charlie was very amused by this. He would also often tell a true story about a married couple who were always quarrelling. Eventually the wife decided to leave her husband and demanded half of their belongings. The poor man was dividing them up and became so flustered that when he came to the ciock he asked her which part she wanted – the morning or afternoon!

Bill West, another roadman, was such a speed merchant on his old bicycle, going down to the station and waving to the passengers on the Northampton train as it started on its journey, only to be waiting for it to arrive at Northampton twenty miles away! Some going on an old upright bike. One evening I was hobbling along on crutches after an accident when he struck me from the rear at a break-neck speed, putting me back to bed for a day or two.

Herbert Maycock, the last of the three, was very touchy whenever rabbit pie was mentioned and would strike out at the person who knowingly pulled his leg. The story goes that his brother arrived home before Herbert on one occasion when they were both single and very carefully lifted the crust of the pie which was waiting for them, eating the rabbit contents and then replacing the crust – quite a shock for Herbert when he cut into it for his supper!

These three men were all staunch Non-conformists and lay preachers and kept our village and approach roads so neat and well mown. They were all experts with the scythe and the grass would look as though it had been cut with a lawn mower. The village was such a credit to this conscientious, God-fearing trio of hard-working men. How different things are today, with the mechanical road-sweeper hurrying through the village and departing in a cloud of dust. I swear the roads are worse for their visits with paper and plastic swept from the gutter and deposited in the centre of the road. This is very noticeable when a detour is made around parked cars. Thank goodness we are lucky to have a kindly farmer named David Kemp nearby, who voluntarily mows our village greens, etc. We are also fortunate to have a couple of men, namely Dick Atterbury and Bill Evans, who keep the Cross Tree and War Memorial immaculate, a veritable show-piece, with flower-beds so tastefully planted and tended. They must be good for they have won first prize for the best kept village memorial for the last six years. Well done!

Then there was Percy Jarvis, who not only worked at his trade as a harnessmaker but repaired boots and shoes and discovered he had a flair for repairing wireless sets, starting with the small crystal sets and earphones and graduating over the years to 8-valve monsters which were capable of getting in touch with America. I remember listening to Tommy Farr's World Heavyweight fight coming direct from the USA in the early hours of the morning – wonderful!

Percy was a remarkable man. He joined the army in the First World War and was a driver of one of the first tanks. I have seen a war correspondent's photo of one of these wedge-shaped monsters, bogged down during an attack, and there, standing all forlorn with his hands in his pockets, was our saddler. I know how thrilled he was after the Second World War when, on going down to the tank museum at Bovington, he saw to his surprise, in pride of place and surrounded by modern marvels, his First World War tank, 'The Hyacinth', his faithful companion, displayed for all to see and marvel at.

Percy was a keen motor cyclist, and in later years became a pedal cyclist, riding a dropped handlebar racing cycle well into his eighties. Then, towards the end of his life, he discovered he was quite a gifted artist. We have an oil painting which he gave us, a country scene, showing two horses at plough, the background being the village of his birth, Brailes. I often look at this painting and wonder what he might have achieved if the 1914–1918 war had not come along. He had such a wealth of latent talent.

Another remarkably gifted man living in our village was a retired schoolmaster, Mr H.O. Roberts, who, with such skill and painstaking care, constructed a beautiful, illuminated record of the village people as they passed away, a most unusual lasting remembrance book, enabling future generations to trace their ancestors with ease. Mr Roberts told me that if he made a mistake on a single page, it took two days to put right. I am sure that a lot of people must think that because of the perfection of this work it must consist of transfers, but not a bit of it. The work is all hand done by a craftsman whom you could imagine illustrating the vellum scrolls of the Middle Ages.

Village life in my young days, when work was done and you had time off, was often centred around the very pretty railway station which was beautifully kept with flower and rose bedecked gardens – the pride of Station Master Trenfield and his staff. They nearly always won the best-kept station competition which was held yearly, or came second. Travelling by train was a very cheap and easy exit to the outside world. Sunday expeditions to the seaside for 5/–(25p) return, were very popular, nearly emptying the village on those Sundays when these trips were made.

The signal box was not always used for the purpose for which it was built. In between pulling off signals and changing the single line right-of-way staff, a signalman would cut our hair for a few coppers. This meant company for him on long winter nights and somewhere warm for his customers to congregate. One signalman was the village bookmaker. Bill would slip out to collect betting slips from the pubs and club, being alerted from his half-pint and various transactions by the Stratford-upon-Avon train giving him several long blasts on the engine's whistle, giving our bookies runner signalman time to rush out of the pub, jump on his bike and get to the signal box in time to pull off the signals to allow the train to continue on its journey.

When this railway track was first completed it was known as the East and West Junction (most unusual for a line to run east to west), but the name was changed at a later date to the South Midland Railway (SMJ) for short, and nicknamed the Slow, Miserable and Jolty! I preferred to think of it as the garden line, as the tracks ran through small stations with colourful flower-beds very like ours, and on to the horticultural valley of Evesham, returning with masses of flowers, fruit and vegetables destined for the cities.

There was a very steep incline out of our station and I have lain in bed listening to heavily laden goods trains huffing and puffing in order to breast this steep rise, the huffs and puffs getting slower and slower. I would hold my breath and wonder whether it could possibly make it, but then, with one almighty puff the train overcame the obstacle and could be heard picking up speed and rattling along on its way.

So many of the railway men were good gardeners, and numerous prizes would be won at the village Flower Show, some more than their garden plots would warrant, and some, I am sorry to say, aided and abetted by their mates, who passed on produce grown in the fertile valleys through which their train ran, all done, no doubt, in good fun.

Our village even boasted a dentist, one Felix Robinson, who would whip out a tooth at any time. In fact, he would break off his evening relaxation over a drink to help a sufferer, and all for the princely sum of 2/6d (25p) a tooth.

I remember one old man named Eli Blower coming to my garage and asking if I had a pair of pointed nosed pliers.

'Yes,' I said, 'here they are – bring them back when you've finished with them.'

'I don't want to take them away,' he said, 'I want you to pull out this tooth.'

I examined the offending molar then placed one hand on top of his head, grasped the tooth with the pliers and pulled hard. After two attempts the tooth shot out and on to the floor and Eli picked it up as he spluttered and spat. I had saved him 2/6d (25p)! I had some misgivings about the sterility of the pliers, and hoped there would be no ill effects, but, as it happened, all was well.

We had two family butchers named Montgomery, who were cousins. Both had shops that were well patronised by the village people and also by neighbouring villages. I helped slaughter for both of them in turn. My job was to go with father and son from one shop on a Monday to collect and drive home a bullock or heifer, usually from a farm in Church Charwelton. It was no easy task to drive a young animal on its own for about three miles, especially if it had a strong desire to get back to the herd. The poor beast would then be shut up and fasted until Wednesday, when I would return to help with its slaughter.

It was a revolting job in those days as the poor beast would be roped by the head, pulled down to an iron ring in the floor until it was on its knees, and then, before the coming and use of humane killers, pole-axed! When the animal was dead, the carcass would be pulled up by its hind feet to the roof, dressed and cut up. My pay for this was 2/6d (25p) and I think I earned it – I would not undertake this work in these more enlightened days for a thousand times that amount.

I often smile when I think of our two children, Denis and Susan, as they watched the dissecting of the twenty score pig we shared with another villager. The cutting up was done at night in our old Salvation Army barracks where the children waited with great expectation for the pig killer to arrive. They would then squat down, whispering to one another and naughtily mocking the man of the moment, who had a peculiar habit of snorting loudly every few seconds. What with the snorting of the children and the pig killer, I half expected the poor dead pig to join in! The children didn't blink an eye when Horace Freeman, the man responsible for the killing and cutting up, whipped out a pig's eye, resting it on a newspaper to show them how it magnified the print. There would be lots of interest shown as he explained that nothing was wasted on a pig, not even the squeal, as this was put into a rubber balloon and could be heard when the balloon was let down – or so he said!

The children would come with us down to the cellar with its built-in salting trough, and speak knowingly about saltpetre and brown sugar, etc. Afterwards, they would sit in front of the fire whilst we talked, over a drink or two, about pigs in the past and those to come, taking everything in their stride.

When the huge side of bacon was hung up in the kitchen on its wall rack (described by the old village folk as the best picture in the house), and we started to cut it up for frying, it was nearly all fat with just a thin streak of lean. My wife would cook some for my breakfast at about 6.30 am after I returned from an early morning start. She would put two thick rashers of bacon in the pan, adding two eggs supplied by our own hens, and these, when cooked, she would place on a large plate for Susan and me. Susan would draw up a stool and stand on it, calmly eating fat bacon and egg and helping to polish the plate with bread, bacon fat glistening on her mouth. No wonder her mother could wrap her up in thick clothes with a large scarf tied round her chest and pinned at the back until she looked as round as she was tall so that, with a happy, rosy face, she was able to play outside in the coldest of weather. When I look at this daughter of ours, with her willowy figure that many a young girl would covet, her beautiful pale complexion and lovely dark eyes, I think to myself, a bit of fat bacon never hurt you, my girl, although I know that you would shudder at the thought of it nowadays. Our son laughs when he asks her if she remembers the pig-killing days and Horace Freeman.

Getting back to my youth, I would go on a Tuesday with the other Montgomery to Eydon and drive, or more often than not, load five or six sheep into the van. I helped very little with the slaughter of these as the butcher had in his employ a disgruntled slaughterer named Harry Hyde, who shunned help. Harry came from a good family but for one reason or another had opted out of the usual lifestyle, and was a loner, sleeping rough on the hay in the loft over the slaughter house.

We also had another character who slept in a loft for years. This was above the bakehouse, so he slept snug and warm. His name was Billy Sewell, the last of a long family line of castrators. Like his family before him, he used no modern methods when doctoring the poor animals – just a sharp knife and his teeth, incessantly chewing tobacco which, he said, acted as a disinfectant. It was the practice to dock puppies tales by biting them off, the distance being measured by the castrator's nose – long nose, long tail, short nose, short tail! What a blessing it was when this practice was outlawed and more humane methods were used.

Living in our village for a number of years was a rather more up-market type of man. He had been educated at a well-known public school and had served in the Brigade of Guards, was very well-spoken and had obviously come from a good family. He had adopted the role of a smallholder and lived in an old derelict mill. He was a very pleasant, plausible fellow, but was so out of character with the villagers that he was given a wide berth by most of them, who watched with interest his wheeler-dealing. We called him 'Electric Whiskers', on account of his large RAF-type moustache.

In spite of, or because of, his education, I don't know which, his smallholding began to run into difficulties and he on to hard times. All kinds of schemes were thought up by him in order to keep his head above water and his daily thirst for beer satiated. One of his tricks, I thought, was well thought out, and it paid off. One day, when in his cups, he told me how he had received payment three times over for a field of cabbages. He first of all sold them, still standing in the field, to a wholesale grocer in Coventry. He then sold them to a merchant in Banbury, receiving ready cash for both of these transactions. On his way home from the pub that night he let his neighbour's cow into the field for a midnight feast, claiming compensation from his neighbour next day for the damage done. He then apologised to both greengrocers for their loss, assuring them that it was beyond his control!

So many of his plans to get rich quick back-fired on him. One of the mad-brained schemes he often employed was to go by bus to a neighbouring town, find an antique shop and carefully select some article or other. He would then bargain with the owner and, if possible, make a deal at a greatly reduced price. Armed with his new possession he would try and sell it to another antique dealer, spinning him a yarn about the greatly reduced circumstances of an old aunt, etc., etc., and hoping his appearance and Guards tie would do the trick. Sometimes it did, but sometimes it did not. Then the object would have to be brought home and hawked around the village with very little success – everyone was wary of Electric Whiskers, our bogus squire.

You will remember that I told you about old Peter Brookes in an earlier chapter – the man who stood on his head and refused to come down – and who would also, at odd times, follow me about asking me to kill him in one way or another, to put him out of his misery. Well, Peter was a dab hand at dealing – I have never seen the like. One day, our aristocratic bogus squire was seen in earnest conversation with Peter. They were constant companions for days on end, putting their heads together, whispering and looking very cunning. The opinion of the villagers was that old Peter had better look out or Electric Whiskers would do it across him. I had other ideas.

'No,' I said, 'Peter will win this battle of shady deals,' and so it proved.

One day Electric Whiskers confided in me. 'Do you know,' he said, 'that damned old Peter has done me in a fashion.'

'I knew he would,' I replied. 'Peter's secret is that he sells before he buys, whereas you buy before you sell, sometimes not selling at all.' We were very proud of the way our village-born man bettered this well-spoken, public-school educated trickster.

Electric Whiskers became more impoverished as time went on and he had to earn a living for a period as a farm worker. He made an odd figure, trudging home from work wet through, with an old sack tied round his waist and another over his head and shoulders as protection against the weather. A far cry from his origins. He once told me that if birth control had been invented earlier he would not be here now! Shortly after this he disappeared. The next time I came across him he was sitting in front of a roaring fire in the lounge of a popular hotel with a large whisky at his elbow. We greeted one another and he put his finger to his lips, signalling to me to be quiet, which, of course, I was, when in walked mine host who greeted me with, 'Oh, you know the squire, then?' Obviously the 'squire's' family had relented, or his dealing methods had improved. All's well that ends well!

I have not mentioned the young farmers in our district, and you might get the impression that their behaviour was impeccable, but not a bit of it – the pranks and horseplay of some of them over the years would fill a book. I recall how the practical joke of one of them changed the name of one of our village pubs for some years afterwards. The name of my farmer friend was Billy Powell, and what a leg-puller he was! He was known far and wide for his tricks, and to illustrate his popularity, I will relate a funny little incident. It was like this:

One day my wife and my mother asked me to take them into Northampton and leave them there to do a day's shopping. I felt I couldn't really spare the time from work and made the journey feeling rather disgruntled. On reaching Northampton I parked with a flourish on the market place car-park which was almost free of cars, and hurried my passengers out, arranging to meet them at 5 o'clock. I then put my car into reverse gear, moving back at a fast pace, when, bang! I came into contact with a stationary car. I got out to inspect the damage and when I saw water streaming out of its radiator, I thought, 'Oh dear, that'll cost me a new radiator.' I was confronted by the other driver who was looking ruefully at his leaking car.

'I shall want your name and address,' he said. 'Where do you come from?' 'Byfield,' I replied.

'Byfield,' he repeated, 'do you know Billy Powell?'

'Oh yes,' I said, 'he is a friend of mine.'

'We'll say no more about it,' said the owner of the car. 'A friend of Billy Powell's is a friend of mine – anyway,

I was a damned fool to pull up behind you when I had the choice of an empty car-park.' Such was the respect county-wide for Billy Powell.

How Billy's tricks almost changed the name of one of our village pubs happened like this. One day one of my lorries ran over a duck belonging to Cecil Cockerell. Cecil, on hearing the brakes of the lorry squeal, came out of his house to see what had happened. He picked up the dead duck and threw it on the muck-heap, saying, 'This will cost Denis a pint when I see him.' I duly paid up and the matter was forgotten. Not so by Billy Powell who, several nights later, removed the duck from its smelly resting place and, making his way to the New Inn, stealthily opened the kitchen door at the back of the pub and placed the bedraggled duck on the table. On entering the bar through the front door and greeting the landlord, Jim Berrill, a retired time-serving quartermaster Marine, who suffered from gout and was a crusty tempered fellow, Billy said, with a twinkle in his eye, 'Have a look on your kitchen table.' Jim disappeared, returning with a smile on his face.

'How much do I owe you, Bill?'

'That's all right – I'll just have a drop of whisky,' our benevolent farmer replied. After two or three free whiskies, he wished Jim goodnight and made his way home.

Several days later the postman delivered a strange parcel to Mrs Powell, and on opening it, she found a foul-smelling bird inside. She threw it on to the yard, chastising Billy when he came in and blaming him for the prank. Once again Billy rescued the poor bird, packed it up and sent it by Express Delivery back to the New Inn. Express Deliveries have to be signed for, so Jim, the landlord, had to accept this suspicious-looking parcel. And so the duck travelled back and forth, thrown through Billy's front door and hidden in strategic places in the pub. The village men entered into the spirit of this grim saga, wondering where next the old duck would turn up. I helped the joke along by painting, on a very large square of cardboard in Old English lettering a foot tall, the sign YE OLDE DUCK INN. I also drew and painted a duck cruising on a pond, its beak emitting large quacks, and to finish the sign off I added a postman in the corner, looking remarkably like Billy Powell.

Pleased with my handiwork, I quietly parked a bus in front of the New Inn at five o'clock the following morning. Then, standing on the bus roof, I fixed up my new sign between the bedroom windows and the front door. This new sign was not noticed by mine host all that day and night and as the regular patrons filed in they all asked Jim if he had changed the name of the pub. This question was asked so many times that Jim became cross and agitated, especially when some of his customers entered the pub quacking loudly.

To make matters worse, poor Mrs Berrill was upset because her hens would not go in to roost for the night, and she asked for help to drive them into the hen-house, but all to no avail. In desperation she opened the roost door in an attempt to get them in that way, only to discover that someone had placed a dead fox just inside with its nose pointing out of the hen-house trapdoor. No wonder the hens were reluctant to roost. Bill Powell was, of course, blamed – who else? and was barred that night from the pub. His closest friend and crony, Alf North, left with him, dropping an explosive crow-scarer on to the fire on his way out. This exploded after they had gone, showering the room with coal and bringing down masses of soot from the chimney. The remaining customers, their glasses, the walls and ceiling, in fact, the whole pub, were absolutely covered in soot and dust, especially the landlord.

The next morning I saw Jim leaning out of the bedroom window with a long broom in his hands trying to remove the Duck Inn sign. He was eventually successful in doing so, but the pub was known far and wide for years as 'The Old Duck'.

Billy, some time afterwards, decided to leave this area and took a farm some distance away. Many were sad to see him go, but many more breathed a sigh of relief, and among them, I am sure, was mine host from the New Inn.

Chapter 20

Set them nobly in the steeple,
Let our bells be rung on high,
There fulfil their heavenly mission,
Midway 'twixt the earth and sky.

When our children ask me how much more I think I can write about yester-year, I tell them I am ready to finish now as they will all be fed up to the teeth with my non-sense. Our son, who is a history professor and the author of a considerable number of biographies including *Radical Joe: A Life of Joseph Chamberlain*, *Prince Philip*, *George VI*, *Lord Reading*, historical and military studies, books for children and two novels, tells me, 'You can't stop now, Dad. You are reaching the time of the Second World War, the most dramatic event of your adult lifetime – you must write on.' Our daughter and grandchildren also encourage me to carry on, and one granddaughter keeps advising me to 'Keep it lively, Gramp, we love it!' But no, I have made up my mind that, for the time being, enough is enough.

Gardening time is almost here when, I like to think, my wife and I help to keep our beautiful country village aspect refurbished for another year by growing masses of flowers – flower power as some people think.

One local inhabitant, an old man and a veteran of the First World War, once said to me that wars would be fun if they fought with pigs' bladders tied on sticks and it was time to call it a day when the bladders burst, and when I stand and look at our village war memorial, count the names on it and recall some of the brave men who gave their all in two world wars, I think my old man with the bladder on a stick idea was so right.

I have a feeling of sadness, as I am sure others have had before me, when I look at and think about the villages I have known and loved. Village life is changing so rapidly nowadays with the building of the motorways, just as it did in Roman times when the Romans brought change to our country by building their roads 2,000 years ago in order to move their legions upon us.

The modern-day legions descend on our houses as old inhabitants die. These homes change hands over and over again in the space of a few years, nearly all to newcomers who can afford to give inflated prices for property for perhaps a year, or possibly two, of residence. We no sooner discover their names than they are off.

New estates spring up in the paddocks and orchards we knew so well. Ancient barns succumb to developers, railway stations, schools, chapels, shops and pubs disappear in the insatiable quest for building space, and the sad thing is we stand by powerless to stem the tide.

When thinking of the motor car and the effect it has had on rural life, and the constant changes in the shape and growth of the villages, I remember what I have been told about the villages that have vanished from around us. They are now just names of fields, or sometimes of large houses or manors, some lived in and others deserted. The signposts point to Appletree, Fawsley, Edgecote, Trafford and Church Charwelton, to name but a few. I am told that eighty villages disappeared from our county alone.

All these village sites were so well chosen, providing shelter from the winter storms and usually watered by a brook strong enough to drive a mill. There were beautiful hillsides and valleys to soak up the summer sun, all sadly to be overrun by countless sheep. When I drive past these sites and look at the mounds and hollows that betray their past existence, I can only wonder if, should the tide of new dwellers continue to pour in from the cities, all that will remain of some of our villages will be supermarket stores and carparks.

If sheep are blamed for the disappearance of village communities in days gone by, how easy it would be for that idol of the twentieth century, the motor car, to have the same effect.

Not many years ago I knew every house and cottage in our village and the people living in them – they were my friends. I knew every child by name and this also applied to the dogs of the village. I also recognised every cycle propped against shop or pub. Now I stand and look at the young mothers passing my gate at school times, some walking but most driving by in cars to pick up or set down their children, and only about one in ten is known to me.

I sometimes stop and look at the children as they stream out of the school in pairs in crocodile formation, all chattering away like magpies on their way either to the playing field for sports and games practice, or to church, or sometimes on nature walks, and I think to myself as I fail to recognise more than a few of the descendants of the old villagers, thank goodness for the children of newcomers, otherwise the village school would be closed and the little ones taken by bus to the nearest town. Some of them, I feel, are far too young to be away all day.

Our village school has shown excellent results over the years and has been fortunate enough to have some very dedicated teachers in its time. One, John Andrews, whose house I bought nearly fifty years ago after he passed on, is so often spoken of with great affection by the senior members of our community. He was headmaster and choir-master from 1896–1933, instilling the pleasures of music, gardening and, above all, cricket, into his pupils and villagers alike.

One disadvantage of the modern mode of village life is that most people, and I don't blame them too much, jump into their cars and journey off to the supermarkets in the nearby towns, coming home with the week's supply of provisions. I know this makes a nice outing for them and the food is cheaper at times than that supplied by the village tradesmen, but it does have an adverse effect on the neighbourhood.

For instance, we had a wonderful grocery store owned by the Russell family who, apart from groceries, stocked and supplied hardware, medical remedies, beer, wines and spirits among many other goods. They also baked bread which they sold in the shop and delivered to the outlying farms in the area. Another of their services which was much appreciated was the baking of Sunday dinners for many of the villagers. In addition to all this they were coal merchants and sold and delivered paraffin for heating and lighting purposes. Unfortunately, this hive of industry gradually faded away with the changing pattern of village life. The old shop has changed hands several times and other types of businesses have been tried but without, it would seem, much success. At the moment a young couple are trying a new venture there, selling carpets. I wish them well. My wife and I often comment, when stuck for some household item – bring Russells back. We were able to get everything there.

One old rural trade that does seem to have taken a new lease of life after fading almost completely away is that of the blacksmith. Nowadays, young men with mobile vans equipped with a forge and welding gear, travel to farms and stables and do the work on the spot. Not a bad idea, and it seems to cope quite adequately with the growing numbers of ponies bought by the newcomers for their daughters. But I must admit, it's not so pleasant as in the olden days when we boys looked over the blacksmith's stabledoor in the evening light and watched that mighty man striking the white hot iron, showering the whole forge with molten sparks. It was nearly as entertaining as a fireworks display. The warm blacksmith's shop was also a haven for some of the old men of the village and those who had been sent home from the farms because of the inclement weather. How they appreciated the shelter and warmth of the forge.

During the winter months when the frost was very severe and ice covered the roads, making it very difficult for the poor horses to stand up, you would see a steady stream of working horses, used for the collection and delivery of milk and goods of all kinds, making their way to the blacksmith's shop to have their sharp triangular frost nails screwed into their shoes. What bustling, busy mornings they were for the smith.

I remember talking to an old man, one John Townsend, who was the last of a long line of blacksmiths of that name. I asked him if he had always worked in Byfield, to which he replied, 'No, not all the time. I was one of a large family of boys. There were too many of us to find work at home, so I ventured out to find work as a blacksmith elsewhere, but this was not an easy task as most blacksmiths' shops were family businesses and they usually had plenty of sons. I walked the roads for miles without much success. Then one day, I was approaching a small village when I heard the ring of a hammer on an anvil. I made my way towards the sound and looking in at the door I asked the fat old blacksmith if there was any chance of a job. "How good are you?" he asked. "I can turn my hand to most things in this trade," I said. "Well, young fellow," said the smith, "do you think you can make me a wink-wank? If so, make it while I go home for my dinner." '

'I took off my jacket,' said John, 'I blew the forge fire until the heat was terrible, then I collected every tool I could find, placing them into the fire, and when they were white hot I took them out and hammered them all together into a molten mass. When the smith returned, he said, "I heard you at work – have you made the wink-wank?" "Yes," I answered, throwing the mass of ruined tools on to the ground, "there's your bloody wink-wank," and I turned and made my way out of his forge and out of the village. How my father laughed when I told him about the wink-wank.'

Another service to the community which goes on unceasing and unchanged over the centuries is the ringing of the church bells – well, it does if you have a dedicated captain of the tower like my friend Fred Hutt. He tells me that the earliest information he has on bell-ringing in our church is that in the year 1552 there were three bells and a Sanctus bell, and that in those days of long working hours when there were very few clocks, bells were relied upon to give some indication of the time of day. Fred says a bell was rung daily at 4 am and 8 pm, for which the clerk responsible received twenty shillings yearly – a mere pittance for getting up before 4 am seven days a week.

Church bells have a pleasant and often well-remembered haunting sound, retained in your memory from childhood days. I recall coming away from an art exhibition held in the village school one afternoon and chatting to Percy Jarvis (our retired harnessmaker), who had shown several of his paintings. Percy by now was an old man, and I asked him about the tune Brailes church bells played at 4 pm each day. He told me, adding that they also rang at 8 am daily, and that he would love to record them.

'Say no more, Percy,' I said, 'my wife and I will pick you up tomorrow and take you to Brailes.'

We duly collected him the next day and spent a very pleasant afternoon touring his picturesque Warwickshire cum north Oxfordshire homeland. At 3.45 pm we were stationed in the churchyard with Percy's tape recorder positioned in a favourable place, and he switched it on when the hand of the church clock pointed to 4 pm. I held my breath and hoped one of those screaming fighter planes would not fly over on manoeuvres shattering the peace, but all was well and Percy recorded his beautiful bells perfectly. He told me afterwards what pleasure this recording gave him when he played it back. I am so pleased we made this happy trip for not long after it, Percy faded away. Our village bells were recorded by the BBC Radio 4, on Sunday, November 6th, 1983, in the programme 'Church Bells on Sunday'. Our ringers, under the guiding influence of Fred Hutt, the tower captain, rang the Kent Treble Bob Minor, and many people wrote to say that they had heard their old village church bells for the first time in years.

When our daughter and her family lived and worked in America for several years, she very skilfully worked out the time gap between America and England, and just as my wife and I were lifting our glasses to toast the New Year to the sound of the bells, the telephone rang and over the line came cheerful voices wishing us a Happy New Year and asking if they had got the time right. I opened the windows and doors and the sound of Byfield bells ringing in the New Year was heard in the USA. I don't think any of us had dry eyes.

It is the custom in our village, and has been for many generations – I could say centuries – to ring the old year out and the new year in. This is a jolly occasion, with the ringers taking refreshment at intervals from a special large earthenware jug, manufactured by our local potter and named the Byfield Ringers Jug. If refreshment is taken too early in the evening, the ringing goes on and on and one year it was 2.15 am before the jug ran dry. The Byfield Ringers Doxology is sung to end the event, when the good people of the village can turn over in their beds and go to sleep.

One village character named Jack (Gadget) Haynes was a very keen ringer, and for years was a great help to Fred Hutt in getting the bells ringing again after the Second

World War, when Fred returned home from serving in the armed forces. Jack, who was himself a veteran of the First World War, serving at Gallipoli, had an enormous bell attached to his bike, which he struck with a six inch nail at different angles, making a merry tune which gave warning of his imminent arrival. I never saw Jack without a large, and I mean large, bunch of flowers on his person, either in his buttonhole or his cap – a very colourful individual.

Our children, after visiting us, are usually loading up their car in readiness for the journey home on a Sunday evening, when the bells ring out for the evening church service. They pause in their departure and listen in silence for a time, taking deep breaths and remarking that the bells sound lovely and the air is like wine.

I started my life and began my story of a Northamptonshire boy with the sound of Little Houghton church bells ringing out. How fitting it will be if I finish my story with bells in mind. They have always appealed to me – I can think of nothing more peaceful than sitting in the garden on a Sunday evening listening to the music of the bells echoing back and forth from the hills around us.

When the time comes for me to lay my bones down in this beautiful Northamptonshire countryside, and this, I hope, will not happen for some time yet, as I have no desire to hasten the inevitable, and when my spirit rises to the sound of our beloved Byfield bells calling their message for all to hear, I will look down upon my loving wife and my beloved children and grandchildren and think what a fortunate man I have been to have had and loved you all, and to have lived my life as a Northamptonshire lad.

We call from tower and steeple
Upon this day of days,
All faithful Christian people to worship
With prayer and praise.
We ring with joyous gladness when man and wife
Are blessed.
We peal in muffled sadness for loved ones
Laid at rest.

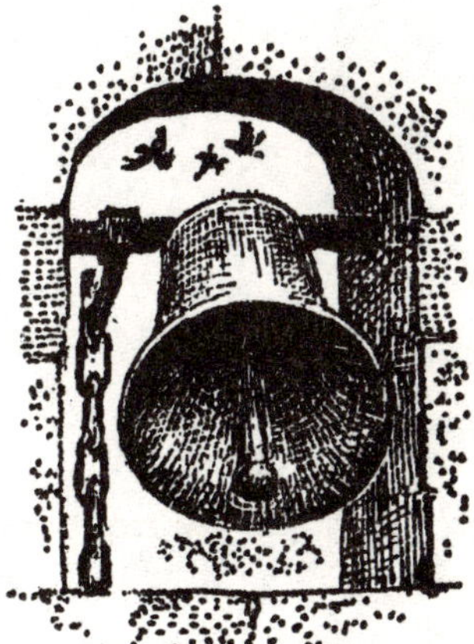